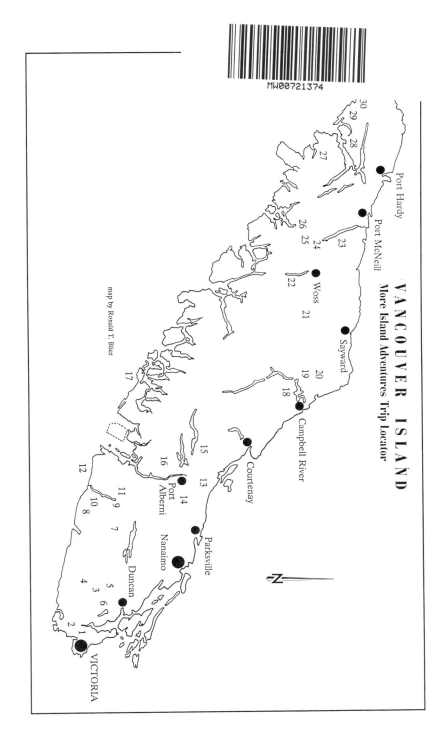

VANCOUVER ISLAND

More Island Adventures Trip Locator

map by Ronald T. Blier

Port Hardy

Port McNeill

Woss

Sayward

Campbell River

Courtenay

Parksville

Port Alberni

Nanaimo

Duncan

VICTORIA

N

30
29
28
27
26
25
24
23
22
21
20
19
18
17
16
15
14
13
12
11
10
9
8
7
6
5
4
3
2
1

More ISLAND ADVENTURES
Volume 2

An Outdoors Guide to Vancouver Island

Richard K. Blier

ORCA BOOK PUBLISHERS

Canadian Cataloguing in Publication Data
Blier, Richard K., 1952–
    More island adventures

    Includes index.
    ISBN 0-920501-91-5
    1. Vancouver Island (B.C.)—Guidebooks.   I. Title.
FC3844.2.B632 1993   917.11'2044   C93-091117-2
F1089.V3B632 1993

Cover design by Susan Fergusson
Maps by R.T. Blier
Photographs by the author, unless otherwise credited

Although every effort has been made to insure that facts presented in this book are accurate and up-to-date, the author and publisher make no guarantee as to the accuracy of information contained herein. Likewise, the author and publisher assume no responsibility for injury or damage to one's person or vehicle resulting from travel in areas described in this book. Go prepared for wilderness conditions and use common sense. Know your personal limitations and your vehicle's capabilities.

Orca Book Publishers
P.O. Box 5626, Station B
Victoria, BC   V8R 6S4
Canada

Printed and bound in Canada

More Island Adventures
is dedicated to Alex—
an authentic individual

Acknowledgements

The author wishes to thank the following persons whose timely and indispensable assistance helped create this book. For aid in compiling the mileages: Frank Bannard, R.T. Blier, Jon Chant, Martin Clegg, Chris Daniel, Tom Ebbs, Peter Geary, Reg Geary, Bill Hadden, Tom Klatt, Ken McDonald, Graeme McFadyen, Riley McFadyen, Wilf Marquis, Martin Nicholas, Timothy Oldford, Dave Palmer-Stone, Colin Prudhon, Alex Semple, Joel Smirl, Dave van Rees and M.L. Wightman. Thanks to the people at regional tourist bureaus, B.C. government offices and logging companies for their time and valuable information. Thanks to R.T. Blier for his maps; Bill Hadden and Jon Chant for photo submissions; M.L. Wightman for secretarial duties and Reg Geary for maintaining my vehicle in logging-road readiness. Proofreading: Jon Chant, Chris Daniel, Tom Ebbs and Dave Palmer-Stone. Word-processing assistance: Brenda Gerth, Angelie VanderByl. Thanks to Frodo's Fotos for photography service and co-operation as the deadline approached. Special thanks to Bob Tyrrell and the staff at Orca Book Publishers for supporting this project.

CONTENTS

About This Book

More Island Adventures, like its companion volume, *Island Adventures*, describes dozens of backroading, hiking, canoeing, camping, fishing and outdoor destinations from the north end of Vancouver Island to the southern tip. These include wilderness lakes, scenic trails, B.C. Forest Service and logging company campsites, wilderness sites and serviced (and unserviced) provincial parks. Vehicular access is via logging mainlines and rougher secondary roads. Some of the thirty trips in this book describe areas that can only be reached by foot or by water. A few trips overlap from book to book. In these cases I refer you to the pertinent chapters in *Island Adventures* where more detailed descriptions of the areas can be found.

Each trip is divided into six sections:

1. *In Brief*: This section includes a short mention of what to expect and notes key points of interest.

2. *Access*: For quick reference, this section lists major access routes for each trip and information on road conditions and possible entry restrictions.

3. *Description*: This detailed section provides distances in kilometres and miles and includes background information with suggestions on area explorations. Important intersections, points of interest and access roads are included.

4. *Contacts*: This section tells who to contact for pertinent details on regional access restrictions and road conditions, updates on hauling roads and active logging areas. Visitors should also check with local chambers of commerce and tourist information centres for additional information.

5. *Maps/Guides*: Relevant maps and guides will appear here. You may obtain these items at the addresses listed under Map Sources at the back of the book. The maps included in *More Island Adventures* are for reference purposes only. Always refer to area topographical and road maps when travelling Vancouver Island backroads.

6. *Nearest Services*: This listing tells where to find the closest gas, groceries and other services.

As the first draft of this book evolved, several areas I later included were not on the original trip list. Bearing names like Nasparti, Klaskish, Rugged Mountain, Ahwhichaolta Inlet and Tahsish—Kwois, these pristine regions, while not as well known as the Carmanah or Walbran valleys, are just as vulnerable to the bite of chainsaws. By describing these remote areas, I hope to bring due attention to some of the few remaining wilderness destinations on Vancouver Island.

Every effort has been made to include current addresses and phone numbers. Expect some discrepancies, as these listings frequently change. Slight variances in the mileages may be noted on slippery or frosty roads. No two vehicles are identical and everyone drives differently. Conditions on Vancouver Island logging roads are constantly changing. (Kilometres have been changed to miles by multiplying by 0.621.)

Island Adventuring

Networks of logging roads snake through the backwoods of Vancouver Island, and as most of these industrial roads are open to the public (with some restrictions), access to prime outdoor recreation spots is relatively easy. It pays to be prepared though, as it's not much fun being stranded in the wilds.

Your vehicle should be in good working order. Maintenance items such as motor oil, antifreeze or summer coolant, brake fluid, a set of tools and a repair manual should be standard additions for backwoods browsers. It's an idea to carry extra food, water and warm clothing with you in the event of a mechanical breakdown, especially on day runs when you may not be carrying overnight gear.

Don't forget to gas up if you'll be venturing into remote regions. Good tires will alleviate some of the possibility of a flat. Some people travel with two spare tires, just in case. It's the secondary roads (and some mainlines) that can be in bad shape, with sharp rocks just waiting to pierce or nick your tires. Don't rush on the logging roads. A slower pace is easier on the nerves and tires, and you can enjoy the scenery a lot better.

There are three general classifications of Vancouver Island logging roads: restricted access, combined-use, and inactive roads. Some routes are signposted as Private Industrial Roads. Read and obey all posted notices on any backroad you venture down.

Restricted-access roads (indicated in some areas by a red, octagonal stop sign) run through active logging areas and sometimes include mainlines with heavy hauling activity. The public can journey on these arteries only after working hours on weekdays or on weekends and holidays. Sometimes these routes are closed to the public

Reading maps is a part of Island adventuring.

at all times for security and safety reasons.

Combined-use roads make up the bulk of Vancouver Island back-roads. These arteries are open to the public twenty-four hours a day, but they are frequently used by logging vehicles. Industrial traffic always has the right-of-way on these logging roads. Pull over at the first opportunity and signal your intentions to the other driver: it's appreciated. If you don't fancy dodging loaded logging trucks or company buses, time your journey to after weekday working hours of the loggers. (A yellow, inverted triangle frequently denotes these roads.)

Inactive roads rarely have any logging traffic and are always open to the public. Lack of maintenance and washouts can render these roads rough or impassable, even with a 4 x 4. (These backroads are often marked by a welcoming green circle.)

Bear in mind that Island backroads are susceptible to Nature's capricious whims. Heavy rains can quickly flood and wash away roadbeds. What you travelled last summer without difficulty might be a washboard of potholes and deep puddles following steady rains. Heavy snow can block higher-elevation routes over the winter. Wet weather virtually eliminates any forest-fire hazard. As a result, road maintenance on secondary spurs and seasonally inactive mainlines is not the priority it is in the summer.

Over periods of dry weather, backroads tend to be very dusty. I always keep a good supply of window cleaner and paper towels on hand to use periodically on my vehicle's windows, headlights and taillights. Being sure you can see other travellers and they can see you is a good safety precaution. And remember to travel with your headlights on.

Maps and guides are indispensable on the backroads. Most logging companies publish recreation road maps for their logging divisions. The B.C. Forest Service distributes several pamphlets on their wilderness campsites on Vancouver Island. You usually have to pick up these maps locally at regional offices or area travel information centres. When used in conjunction with area topographical charts, these road guides lessen the chance of becoming lost. Regional marine charts complement any paddling or boating adventure on the Island's inlets. Readers will be pleased to know that maps in the National Topographical Series (1:50,000 scale) are being updated. Some new southern Vancouver Island sheets are already available at local map outlets. I always carry a small notebook along and jot down observations and the mileages for key junctions and turnoffs. It helps when you can delegate this task to your passenger en route, but a steady hand is needed on the bumpy logging roads.

It can be disconcerting to head off to a particular locale only to be thwarted by locked gates, fire closures or impassable roads. A phone call, just prior to your trip, to regional logging company offices or the B.C. Forest Service will update road conditions and any access limitations you may encounter. Talk to your friends. A personal recollection from a backwoods browser often provides hints not included in any guide. Many of my favourite Island hideaways have been discovered simply by inquiring with locals. Some have even revealed hot fishing spots—but only after I have been sworn to secrecy.

Don't forget to tell someone reliable where you're going and when you'll be back. This has proven to be a bit of a problem with me—with the wide choice of wilderness destinations around and the countless, intriguing side roads, I sometimes end up in a slightly different location than the one I originally pinpointed.

Be sure to boil or treat your drinking water, particularly in areas of high use. Many travellers carry an adequate supply of water with them. B.C. Parks warns hikers on popular trails, such as the West Coast Trail and those within Cape Scott Provincial Park, to treat all surface water. Intestinal disorders can play havoc with outdoor activities. One such disease, a parasitic infection of the intestines, called giardiasis, is spread by animal and human waste, and appears to be on the increase.

Over the years, I've developed a few checklists to help in pre-trip planning. These are divided into canoeing, hiking, vehicle camping, tenting and 4 x 4 travel categories. Using prepared lists saves time as you pack and lessens the chance of forgetting some crucial piece of gear. Food lists vary according to personal preference and length and type of trip. Take the time to find a recipe for beef jerky. On

Many Vancouver Island adventurers base camp in a vehicle.

backpacking trips, homemade jerky is a treat, and quite economical.

Many backroad campsites are user-maintained—visitors are expected to clean up their sites before they leave. By practising low-impact camping procedures we can all help preserve the wilderness atmosphere that nowadays can be hard to find.

Off-Season Travel

Many backwoods browsers feel a campground is far too crowded should one or two other campsites be occupied. They will go to great lengths to discover a secluded spot more to their liking. Such elusive hideaways are easier to find in the off-season. Then, even the more popular logging company and B.C. Forest Service campsites (those that consistently fill up over the summer months) are frequently empty.

Always be ready for the worst weather and gear up accordingly. The majority of off-season adventurers base in a camper (or camperette), small trailer or van. Others rough it in the back of a pickup, protected by only a canopy. Some have even been known to scrunch into the confines of a hatchback car, hatch up, with a tarp positioned to ward off the rains. A few still carry only a tent.

Whatever your choice of sleeping accommodations, a good winter sleeping bag is essential, especially if you're not using a small heater unit or comfortably tucked into the warmth of a camper. Nothing will make you swear off the notion of off-season camping quicker than a shivery night of tossing and turning. That sleeping bag you used in August may not do the job in November or March.

I found this out during a late-fall hiking foray on northern Vancouver Island. My trusty down bag had reached the end of the trail. No amount of shaking would restore the insulating loft so essential to warmth. The stitching was going, creating gaps which dissipated any heat my body might generate. I donned several layers of clothing and waited out the night while my travelling partner snored away in comfort, with only his nose poking out from the obviously warm confines of his mummy bag. I'm still not sure what kept me up more effectively—the cold and damp or the sawmill operating a midnight shift in Mike's sleeping bag. Shortly after that trip I invested in the quality synthetic-fibre bag I've been using ever since.

In the off-season, hours of daylight are limited. You're bound to spend parts of your day inside, so pack a good flashlight and extra batteries. I carry a couple of flashlights and spare batteries. Avoid the rechargeables when camping. They are great in town but they do run down quickly in colder temperatures. Candles are handy but should be used with care in a secure holder. You'll be amazed at the amount of heat a candle gives off. Another option is a lantern of some sort, but remember that these contraptions (and portable heaters) require adequate ventilation. Flashlights only in a tent.

Bring foul weather gear—rainproof coat, pants and water-resistant footwear. That way you can spend time outside even if it's showery. You don't want to be cooped up the whole trip. I prefer a Floater coat, rainpants and gum boots for my campsite wanderings. Veteran backwoods browsers know the benefits of layering their clothing in colder weather. As they say, it's the dead air space that insulates. Make sure one of those layers is wool: it'll still keep you warm when wet. Don't forget a hat or toque. Heat loss from an uncovered head can be substantial. Read up on hypothermia (rapid loss of body heat) and watch for the warning signs.

One of the benefits of off-season travel is the lack of bugs. You know the type: voracious mosquitoes, determined deerflies and frenzied no-see-ums that play havoc with summer outings. Luckily, the flying fiends thin out in the spring and fall, and are not a factor over the winter. Still, I always carry some repellent (and some antihistamine lotion) just in case.

Storing perishable food is not a problem. There's no need for ice in your cooler when it's cold out. Natural refrigeration will keep your provisions from spoiling. Before you retire for the evening, or if

In the off-season backwoods browsers often encounter frosty conditions on Vancouver Island backroads.

you're planning to be away from camp for a length of time, make sure any food items are either hung up or secured against hungry varmints or the occasional larger forager. Raccoons are frequent camp visitors, especially at coastal destinations. These nighttime bandits like nothing better than to scavenge through carelessly stored food stashes and backpacks. You can stow a cooler in your vehicle overnight as one safeguard against hungry wildlife.

A large tent fly or tarp roped between trees can easily be set up in camp so you can cook meals out of the rain or simply sit around your campsite. Extra gear can be kept under this makeshift roof. To many campers, no outing is complete without a campfire blazing. How many of us have built a fire on summer jaunts when, really, we could have (and during times of high forest fire hazard, should have) done without one? In the off-season, a campfire is essential; its heat fends off the chill and keeps the coffee water on the boil.

Sometimes, even following periods of dry weather, only damp wood can be found at wilderness campsites. If you've tried to light a fire during a West Coast downpour you know the value of having some sort of firestarter around. (A couple of empty milk containers for your first match can be effective with kindling.)

Many times I've climbed above the freezing line to encounter severe frost or seen what had been a steady rain at lower elevations turn into a sudden fall of snow. As the sun dips to the horizon, or is cut off by imposing mountains, the evening chill seeps in relentlessly. Roads that were bare gravel during the day can frost over rapidly by evening's gloaming. If there's a chance you'll hit freezing temperatures and snow, consider carrying chains with you. And don't forget a small shovel and sand or even kitty litter for traction.

Extended high pressure is rare during the off-season. When it does occur, you can glean an idea of what to expect by watching the long-range forecasts before your journey. You're still likely to have showers somewhere on your wanderings. Unsettled conditions are the norm in the off-season. Don't be afraid to cut short a trip should conditions deteriorate beyond your tolerance. After all, there's always next week.

Cameras and Camping

Whether you're contemplating a rugged wilderness journey or a simple daytrip from your vehicle, there are a few hints and safeguards to consider when carrying a camera along on outings. Normally I carry two cameras and pare down the filters and lenses that may see limited duty. You sometimes have to be a little ruthless with this procedure but it pays off—especially if you plan to lug everything around in a backpack for any length of time. Paddlers have the luxury of including an extra lens or more.

Protection from moisture, rain, dust and those unavoidable bumps and knocks is crucial to all cameras, particularly those with electronic parts. A soft towel, folded into the bottom of a camera case or day pack, will absorb many potentially damaging jolts as you hike around with your gear. A second towel placed on top of your equipment gives additional buffering.

Line your pack with a heavy-duty plastic bag and bring along extra tie-tags to seal it with. (Somehow the twist-ties always seem to go missing during photo breaks.) I separate my cameras, film, lens-cleaning supplies and various lenses into Ziploc bags. Leave in some air to add further cushioning. Into each Ziploc and the camera case it's an idea to put one of those small, silica-gel desiccants to absorb minute moisture. This can be a propitious move when shooting in wet situations. Backup batteries can be safely stored in an empty film canister.

When loading your canoe or kayak, keep your camera handy and ready to go. On big-lake excursions, I stash the camera bag under the spray cover, right in front of me. The Ziplocs and plastic pack liners will isolate your gear from errant spray or rain. Remember to lash your pack to a thwart in the event of a capsize, but make sure such securing doesn't interfere with quick access to your camera. On overnighters or more extensive hiking adventures, keep your photo outfit in an easy-to-get-at section of your pack. No one tosses down their backpack top-first at each rest stop, so it makes sense to stick your camera apparatus in the uppermost compartment. Pad your equipment with some extra clothing for added protection.

Always a dilemma is whether or not the tripod goes along. On shorter jaunts, including your light extender is no real problem, unless it's a real behemoth. On outings of more than a day or so, or when your hike involves arduous trails, a compact, collapsible tripod is ideal. The only problem with some of the lighter models is that they cannot accommodate the weight of the heavier telephoto and zoom lenses. Chances are, any shots captured from a canoe or kayak won't be taken with a tripod even if you do decide to pack one. But there will be times during shoreline explorations when you'll be glad to have one with you. Slipping the tripod under the spray cover next to your camera paraphernalia keeps it accessible and dry. For extra defense against the elements (and your own clumsy handling), you can wrap your tripod with a towel and seal it inside a plastic bag.

Cameras have the annoying tendency to malfunction in cold or damp weather. Under frosty conditions the lubricated parts may stick or seize up, halting any photo sessions. I encountered this problem on a January photo run to northern Vancouver Island. Luckily, I was able to substitute my second camera for the delinquent one. The latter returned to action later after warming up in my vehicle.

If you're still mulling over bringing your camera on an extended trip, break that confining habit and start packing. It's easier than you think to be ready for those great shots you know will be there.

TRIP 1: Highlands Roads

In Brief

Just outside of Victoria is a delightful run through the Highlands district. The route accesses several Capital Regional District (CRD) parks (including Lone Tree Hill, Mount Work and Thomas Francis/Freeman King parks) each with hiking trails. Durrance Lake is a popular swimming and fishing destination.

Access

Take Highway 1 west from Victoria to the Millstream Road intersection in Langford. The route is paved and hard surface (pea gravel and oil).

Description

One of my favourite drives goes through the Highlands, west of Victoria, up to Durrance Lake and over to West Saanich Road. The starting point is easy to find. Take Highway 1 west from Victoria to the Millstream Road intersection in Langford. Turn right onto Millstream Road and reset your vehicle's trip meter to zero.

At km 1.5 (mi 0.9) you'll pass the entrance to Western Speedway and the adjacent waterslide park. Finlayson Arm Road, on the left at km 4.6 (mi 2.9), can be followed all the way to Goldstream Park. (This road is extremely narrow with tight corners. Watch out for oncoming traffic.) At km 5.4 (mi 3.4) the road splits: for this run we stay right on

The Capital Regional District's Lone Tree Hill Park is along Highlands roads.

Millstream Lake Road. But you may decide to keep left on Millstream Road and continue about 2.5 km (1.6 mi) to the CRD's Lone Tree Hill Park. A little before the park is the restored cabin of Caleb Pike, who settled in the region circa 1883. The restoration was completed using original tools from that era, and was sponsored by the Highlands Heritage Park Society.

Lone Tree Hill Park, created in 1983, comprises 31 ha (77 ac). The park is named after a solitary Douglas fir on the summit. The fir is a designated heritage tree and has stood for over two centuries. The elements have battered the tree over the years and the results of Nature's relentless forces show. The tree stands but 4 m (13 ft) high, shrunken and gnarled by wind and rain. Its only neighbour is a single arbutus. Lone Tree Hill (el. 388 m/1273 ft) is part of the Gowlland Range, on the east side of Finlayson Arm.

A trail from the parking lot climbs gently at first, then steepens further along. There are numerous rest spots at key panoramic viewpoints. Avoid scrambling over the delicate vegetation at the top of Lone Tree Hill. People sometimes forget that fragile areas in the forests, meadows and alpine areas of Vancouver Island become more vulnerable as time and increased numbers of people pass by. Always stay on existing trails.

The view from the summit takes in the Highlands and Victoria. To the west the Warwick Range and the Malahat dominate the backdrop. If you look closely (binoculars are handy), you can spot the bustling traffic of the Island Highway on the far side of Finlayson Arm. The imposing shape of Mount Finlayson towers to the south; to the east, Mitchell and Second lakes (two small highland ponds) are visible. The Dominion Astrophysical Observatory, near Prospect Lake, is identifiable. On an exceptionally clear day Haro Strait and San Juan Island make good viewing. A visit to this picturesque CRD hilltop is well worth it.

Millstream Lake Road cuts north at km 6.3 (mi 3.9). To the right the route becomes Munns Road and winds along to Mount Work's southern trailhead near Fork Lake (km 8.3/mi 5.2). You'll eventually hook up with Prospect Lake Road at Thomas Francis/Freeman King Regional Park (km 15.3/mi 9.5). This CRD park features over 11 km (6.8 mi) of trails, including a boardwalk loop—the Elsie King Trail—for the disabled. Here visitors can explore wetlands and rocky hilltops surrounded by majestic fir and cedar. Thomas Francis donated land for public use in 1960; seven years later the City of Victoria gave the province property that comprises Freeman King Park. Management of the land was transferred to the CRD in 1981.

Our Highlands roads jaunt stays on Millstream Lake Road and twists its way by Mitchell, Second and Third lakes, by which time the road is called Durrance Road. Years ago the route was rough gravel and you had to contend with occasional waterholes. The rutted hill near Pease Lake caused problems for those with regular cars, especially if you were heading south. Much of the driving challenge is gone now as the road has been greatly improved and smoothed with pea gravel and oil. At a switchback (km 10.9/mi 6.8) you'll be able to see Pease Lake off to the left. A short trail goes down to the lake at km 11.3 (mi 7). Respect the private property in this area.

You can leave your vehicle at km 11.8 (mi 7.3) and take the Timberman Trail down to McKenzie Bight. The main parking area for the McKenzie Bight Trail (and Mount Work's Summit Trail) is just down the road at km 12.1 (mi 7.5). The trail branches into several paths through the ravine forest as you drop down towards McKenzie Bight. A boisterous waterfall on Cascade Creek is one highlight. The thick canopy of the trees allows limited sunlight onto the forest floor. Swordfern, salal, lichens and mosses thrive in this shadowy environment. Just east of the confluence of Pease and McKenzie creeks the grotto displays evidence of glacial deposits.

Should you prefer a little climbing, take the trail to the summit of Mount Work, the highest point on the Saanich Peninsula (446 m/1463 ft). The north trail to Mount Work's summit is more strenuous than

A *visitor takes in the view at McKenzie Bight*.

the southern route that begins from Munns Road; both have steep sections. You are rewarded for the climb by frequent openings in the forest and stunning vistas. Also of interest is Tolson Pond, so tiny it's not even on area topographical maps. Remember to carry enough water with you. Park regulations prohibit open fires and overnight camping.

At the junction with Willis Point Road (km 12.2/mi 7.6) a left zigs and zags down to Mark Lane which follows the waterfront to pass several coves. The waters here, part of Squally Reach, are popular with divers. Where the road turns rough you can park and hike south to McKenzie Bight.

Turn right for Durrance Lake when you reach Willis Point Road. At km 12.5 (mi 7.8) Durrance Close angles off to the left. From the parking lot you can hike right around the lake. Durrance Lake has good trout and bass fishing as well. One cold winter years ago a friend and I ventured up to the lake to find it frozen over. Someone had shovelled a small patch of ice clear of snow to serve as a skating rink. The next day we returned with our skates and hockey sticks to indulge in a very rare pastime: outdoor hockey.

We came back for three successive days until a sudden warming in the weather cut short our natural-rink hockey season.

A new section of Willis Point Road, south of Durrance Lake and Heals Rifle Range, runs east to Wallace Drive (km 16.2/mi 10.1), just north of Farmington. This connecting link eliminates the traffic delays park-goers and local residents often faced on the old route when the range was in use. The first two switchbacks won't be missed either. The next time you feel like a Sunday drive (or any other day of the week, for that matter), consider a meander along the Highlands roads.

Contacts

CRD Regional Parks Department (604) 478-3344.

Maps/Guides

Various CRD park pamphlets; Guide to the Forestland of Southern Vancouver Island (Lake Cowichan Combined Fire Organization); *Hiking Trails I* (Outdoor Club of Victoria Trails Information Society); *The Naturalist's Guide to the Victoria Region* (Weston & Stirling/Victoria Natural History Society); National Topographical Series: 92B/5 Sooke (1:50,000); 92B/6 Victoria (1:50,000); 92B/11 Sidney (1:50,000); 92B/12 Shawnigan Lake (1:50,000); Provincial Map: 92B/NW Victoria (1:125,000).

Nearest Services

Greater Victoria area.

TRIP 2: Harbourview Road

In Brief

Four-wheel enthusiasts will enjoy a jaunt along the backroads through Sooke Mountain Provincial Park and up to Sheilds and Grassie lakes. A washed-out road can be hiked in to Crabapple Lake. The area is also frequented by mountain bikers.

Access

Take Highway 14 towards Sooke. About 4 km (2.5 mi) west of Gillespie Road (near the 17 Mile House), turn right onto Harbourview Road. From the start of the gravel the road is rough with washouts, waterholes and problematic hills. The route is passable only with a high-slung truck or 4 x 4.

Description

One of the great things about living on Vancouver Island is that you don't have to travel very far to get out in the woods. And one of the areas regularly visited by backwoods browsers—when the gates are open—is reached along Harbourview Road, just east of Sooke. From Victoria, drive west on Highway 14 to Saseenos and turn right onto Harbourview Road. This turn is about 4 km (2.5 mi) west of the Gillespie Road cutoff. (*Island Adventures*: Trip 1.) When you leave the highway, reset your vehicle's trip meter to zero. The start of the gravel is at km 0.7 (mi 0.4). From this point on, a truck or 4 x 4 will be needed.

Vancouver Island is criss-crossed by networks of backroads that lead to wilderness adventure spots.

There is a crossroad just over the 2-km (1.2-mi) mark. Bear left and then make an immediate right up a sometimes slippery hill. The original road here has been eroded by heavy runoff and a deep sinkhole is clearly marked and barricaded by ribboned tree limbs. By km 4 (mi 2.5) a sheer rock face on Mount Manuel Quimper (Mount Shephard) will be visible on the right. Hikers seek out the overgrown arteries that snake up the flanks of this Sooke-area landmark. The region is prime habitat for cougars, who prefer the semi-open terrain. You may also see signs of deer. Red squirrels and many types of birds also live here.

The road swings due east near a viewpoint (km 4.3/mi 2.7). Then comes a rugged hill. At km 5.7 (mi 3.5) is the site of a former washout. Years ago this was the end of the line for many vehicles, as runoff had eaten away the roadbed. A bypass now skirts the problem area. You still have to take it slow at the Charters River crossings near Ragged Mountain. Large rocks and an exposed culvert at the first one still require careful straddling. It helps to have someone guiding you through so you don't scrape your vehicle's undercarriage or get hung up on a protruding rock. The second creek crossing (km 7.7/mi 4.8) has been improved with a log bridge. This site has washed out a number of times. Pavement once extended all the way in to the southern boundary of Sooke Mountain Provincial Park. Most of it is long gone now, but remnants still remain along parts of the route. Watch for these jagged fragments—they can be rough on tires.

The Sheilds Lake/Crabapple Lake junction is at km 8.7 (mi 5.4). Straight ahead runs up to Crabapple Lake, but the severity of the hill precludes most four-wheelers. Hikers and mountain bikers can journey in to Crabapple Lake and beyond to the site of an old fire lookout on Empress Mountain. The view from the top is spectacular. A plethora of confusing side roads makes it easy to get lost. Carry maps and a compass at all times. Of course it's even better to have someone along who knows the area well. Some friends of mine are talking about taking mountain bikes all the way to Empress Mountain. They hope to complete a loop down to Sooke Potholes Provincial Park.

After periods of rain the backroad's potholes and low-lying areas fill up. Some of these water obstacles completely cover the roadway. Once, just for fun, on our way down to Highway 14, we counted as many of the larger waterholes as we could. This was right after a day of heavy rainfall. The results surprised us: 138 relatively deep puddles, with an average of twenty per km (0.6 mi) closer to the lakes. In conditions like these, a shovel, heavy rope and a come-along could come in handy.

Turn left at the 8.7-km (5.4-mi) junction for Sheilds Lake. At km 8.9 (mi 5.5) you will reach the bottom of a steep hill. Cut left and work your way up the grade. The road twists in to the lake and several wilderness campsites. Along this stretch the road dips into a gulley. The short but often slick hill here can be tricky, especially on the way out. A buddy and I once had to build up the road with logs and rocks to get through.

By km 10 (mi 6.2) you'll reach a beautiful wilderness campsite on the north side of Sheilds Lake. The road twists its way west to a fork about 1 km (0.6 mi) away. Straight ahead goes to Grassie Lake. The left road crosses a small stream and peters out at the site of a former scout camp. There are several campsites here close to the west shores of Sheilds Lake. Both Grassie and Sheilds lakes have been stocked with cutthroat trout. The lakes sit at an elevation of about 400 m (1312 ft) and are great fly-casting destinations. Many anglers use belly boats or carry in a small cartop boat or canoe.

A brief mention of Harbourview Road's locked gates is in order. For years only fire closures or impassable road conditions kept Island adventurers out of the region. And then not for long. You had to expect a lot of paint-scratching branches, jarring hills and tricky creek

Harbourview Road is frequently travelled by mountain bikers.

crossings, but the wilderness charm of Sooke Mountain Provincial Park and secluded fishing on area lakes was worth the effort. In the late 1970s, the route was actually improved dramatically by private landowners. At that time I was able to negotiate a late-model Toyota Corolla all the way in to Crabapple Lake. A few years later the gates at the bottom of the road were locked indefinitely.

The problem was that the access road ran through Greater Victoria Water District territory and adjacent private property. Public safety concerns, vandalism, security and litter problems—if you can call wrecked cars and other trash litter—prompted the locked-gate policy. The closure effectively prevented any vehicle from accessing Sooke Mountain Provincial Park and the trout lakes beyond. Hunters, anglers and area backroaders were suddenly barred from their favourite haunts. Trail bikers, hikers and people with mountain bikes weren't thwarted by the closure, though they were open to trespassing charges.

And there the matter rested. Occasional objections would be voiced through phone calls and letters—flickers of disapproval, yet ones that persisted; like the pulsating embers of a dying campfire that refuses to go out, but flares to life with each sporadic gust of wind. At the time of this writing, late 1992, the three gates at the bottom of Harbourview Road had been removed, along with the Water District's Harbourview Dam, but things could change. Let's all do our part in ensuring continued public access to the region. Carry out your trash, follow seasonal fire, hunting and fishing regulations and don't cut trees. Take pride in our Observe, Record and Report Program. Vancouver Islanders are gaining an envied reputation for monitoring their forestlands.

I spoke with a number of other backwoods browsers I met on a run up to Sheilds Lake right after the gates were opened. We swapped quick tales of previous visits and changeable road conditions. We also updated each other on current fishing conditions before continuing our backroad travels. It felt good to be back.

Contacts

B.C. Forest Service (Duncan) (604) 746-2700; B.C. Parks (Victoria) (604) 387-5002; B.C. Parks Public Information Officer (Victoria) (604) 387-4609; Greater Victoria Water District (Victoria) (604) 478-1715.

Maps/Guides

Guide to the Forestland of Southern Vancouver Island (LCCFO); National Topographical Series: 92B/5 Sooke (1:50,000); Provincial Map: 92B/NW Victoria (1:125,000).

Nearest Services

Saseenos; Sooke.

TRIP 3: Weeks Lake to Sooke

In Brief

Island adventurers can travel backroads from the Shawnigan Lake area all the way to Sooke. Most of the route requires a high-slung vehicle or 4 x 4. Weeks Lake is a popular fishing destination.

Access

Take either the South Shawnigan Lake cutoff or the turn in Mill Bay on Highway 1, and travel to the northwest end of Shawnigan Lake and the junction of Renfrew Road and West Shawnigan Lake Road. The mainline, west of Shawnigan Lake, is in good shape. Spur roads are rough and could require a high-slung vehicle or 4 x 4. Continued lack of maintenance and seasonal washouts may render some roads impassable. The region is subject to fire closures. You may encounter active hauling on the mainline, west of Shawnigan Lake.

Description

To reach our starting point, near Shawnigan Lake's West Arm, you can cut off the Trans Canada Highway onto South Shawnigan Lake Road and travel along the east or west side of Shawnigan Lake. The most direct route is over the Malahat to Mill Bay; then head west to the village of Shawnigan Lake and continue around the north end of the lake. (Island Adventures: Trip 5.) Reset your vehicle's trip meter to zero at the junction of West Shawnigan Lake Road and Renfrew Road. At km

Fishing halts for a quick meal of pan-fried trout; then it's back to casting.

1.9 (mi 1.2), Gleneagle Road cuts off on the right. It is along this road that you can access the south end of the Kinsol Trestle. (See Trip 6.) The pavement ends just beyond Gleneagle Road. At the Burnt Bridge crossing (km 5.1/mi 3.2) keep left up the hill. At km 11 (mi 6.8) a hauling road swings off to the left; stay right on the public road to climb a long, steep grade. At the top is a fine viewpoint.

Canadian Pacific Forest Products hauls along the mainline, west of Shawnigan Lake, so watch out for loaded trucks. You may be inclined to time your travels to after weekday working hours. Keep straight ahead at an intersection at km 15.8 (mi 9.8). The Weeks Lake turn is on the left, just over the 19-km (11.8-mi) mark.

Turn left and watch for another road on the left (km 21.6/mi 13.4) that runs down to Weeks Lake. From here the road gets a little rougher. Its severity depends on the time of year, what damage flooded streams have inflicted on the roadway and culvert sites, and how much rock-moving and bridge-building has been done by fellow travellers. Spring and fall anglers sometimes have to dodge waterholes.

A little beyond a gravel pit is the rutted road down to Weeks Lake (km 23.6/mi 14.7). Some days you can roam around Weeks for hours without a strike or sign of fish. You might be able to hook one by dragging a worm along the lake bottom, but that will be all. It's those special days when the lake's surface is speckled with rings that anglers look for. Weeks is regularly stocked with rainbow trout. Cartop boats may be launched at a natural boat ramp.

This viewpoint is along the Weeks Lake-to-Sooke backroads.

My brother and I went in to Weeks one early spring. There was still plenty of snow around at higher elevations and once we reached Weeks Lake, we decided to continue on to Butler Main. We never got through. Heavy snows still lurked in the shadowed valley, just south of the lake. We locked the hubs, put the truck in low ratio and jerked ahead. Someone had been through recently, and it was in the unknown backwoods browser's tire tracks we were now desperately trying to stay. The advantage of a wider-based vehicle with biting treads on its tires became obvious on the first real hill. We managed a U-turn—that was another interesting chore—and backtracked to barer road.

A couple of years later I had an update on the Weeks-to-Butler Main section from an angling buddy whose friend had driven the route the week before. Bill summed it up succinctly with one word: rough. I told him later, after I went through myself, that his friend was right, and could have added rougher and roughest to his report. In the Leech River Valley, just west of Survey Mountain, washout after washout has deteriorated the road. Most of these have been built up with rocks and wood, but there are still a couple of tricky spots.

Next comes a steep, somewhat rutted hill as the road plunges into the valley. Around the 30-km (18.6-mi) mark an old side road on the left runs down to a bridge site on the Leech River. You might want to hike around a bit and take in the river canyons.

At km 31.4 (mi 19.5) a long grade winds up to a viewpoint that, on clear days, features the distant snows of Mount Baker in Washington State. The extent of area logging is dramatically reflected by the stark slopes of Survey Mountain and the ribbons of logging roads clinging to the walls of the Leech River Valley.

You never know what to expect on Vancouver Island backroads. In early April of 1992 I was working my way to Sooke when a strong windstorm hit. The gusts stirred up smouldering slash that flared quickly into a 200-ha (494-ac) wildfire. The smoke was thick overhead when I hit Butler Main. A droning Martin Mars water bomber from Sproat Lake made an appearance as part of the successful fire-fighting effort.

The road then drops down a hill to the Leech River bridge. West Leech Falls are nearby. At km 37.3 (mi 23.2) you'll reach Butler Main, the mainline coming in from Sooke. A jaunt to Bear Creek Reservoir via Butler Main is detailed in Trip 4.

Contacts

Canadian Pacific Forest Products (Cowichan Division) (604) 749-3796; Canadian Pacific Forest Products (Ladysmith) (604) 245-3233; B.C. Forest Service (Duncan) (604) 746-2700.

Maps/Guides

Guide to the Forestland of Southern Vancouver Island (LCCFO); National Topographical Series: 92B/5 Sooke (1:50,000); 92B/12 Shawnigan Lake (1:50,000); Provincial Map: 92B/NW Victoria (1:125,000).

Nearest Services

Shawnigan Lake; Sooke.

TRIP 4: Bear Creek Reservoir

In Brief

A day run in the Sooke Hills always appeals to backwoods browsers. The Butler Main logging road is one gateway to adventure. Some travellers even choose to camp overnight at the wilderness campsites at Bear Creek Reservoir. The fishing here can be good in the spring and fall.

Access

Drive to Sooke and take Otter Point Road to Young Lake Road. Take Young Lake Road to Camp Barnard. Swing right onto Butler Main logging road. The route follows a gravel logging mainline that is in good-to-fair shape with some steep hills. Secondary roads may be overgrown and rough. These may require a 4 x 4. Some older routes may be impassable. The area is subject to seasonal fire closures.

Description

A few years ago a friend of mine was back on the Island—on one of his famous whirlwind tours—and even though his visit was brief, I wasn't going to let him get away without our heading off on the backroads. We decided to go up in the Sooke Hills via Butler Main. (*Island Adventures:* Trip 3.) We cut onto the mainline near Camp Barnard and worked our way up the steep valley directly east of Bluff Mountain. At km 10.5 (mi 6.5) I pointed out the barely discernable

Shoreline fishing can be productive in Island lakes.

side road on the left that leads in to Tugwell Lake. This washed-out spur has been impassable for years. Anglers don't mind. You can still hike up to the lake and shore cast along game trails. Watch out for snags, though. Tree limbs and lakeside bushes have a strong appetite for spoons and spinners. Determined fishermen will carry in a belly boat and cast their way along the lakeshore.

Tugwell Main connects with Butler Main at km 11.7 (mi 7.3). This backroad was once a hauling road and remains a fire-access route, but without regular maintenance its rough stretches are suitable only for a high-slung vehicle or 4 x 4. The gates at the north and south ends are sometimes locked. We found our first swimming hole at km 12.9 (mi 8). Over the summer I've often stopped at this roadside pond for a refreshing dip. Our next stop was at the viewpoint (km 13.8/mi 8.6) that looks out over the Leech River Valley. On a clear day you can gaze eastward to the snowy heights of Mount Baker in Washington State.

At km 15.3 (mi 9.5) the secondary road on the right leads to Weeks Lake and on to the logging road networks west of Shawnigan Lake. (See Trip 3.) We kept straight ahead on the mainline for Bear Creek Reservoir. We detoured once onto a side road at km 17.6 (mi 10.9) that took us through a gravel pit and up onto another road we later identified as Branch W54. We eventually had to shift into low four-wheel as we headed west and continued a climb that brought us into a patch of old growth high atop the ridges east of the reservoir. The road ended in a cutblock with an excellent view of Bear Creek Reservoir off in the distance. We retraced our route and stayed on W54 to emerge back on Butler Main near the Weeks Lake cutoff.

Around the 20-km (12.4-mi) mark Bear Creek Reservoir will be visible on the left. Most of the side roads in this vicinity lead down to primitive campsites on the water. The majority of these roads are rough and prone to mudholes in wet weather. The dips and dives on some of them make it hard to get in with a regular car. We negotiated one of these arteries down to the water and soon had the canoe off-loaded and the tent up.

A relatively dry year had lowered the water level considerably as evidenced by giant stumps protruding out of the water. You could walk around others that were higher up on the bank. Paddlers and boaters should note that whitecapped waves caused by strong winds are often encountered on reservoir waters. In these conditions the sunken stumps, particularly those just below the surface, are potential hazards; it's easy to get hung up. A friend told me he had run aground on one of them and almost capsized his canoe trying to get off. Be cautious out on the water.

Things were calm when we canoed around the reservoir, poking into bays and trying some fishing. Bear Creek Reservoir has been stocked with rainbow trout. They are sometimes wormy over the summer, but they take readily to a fly in late spring and fall. The reservoir sits at an elevation of about 400 m (1312 ft) so the fishing action here comes later and ends earlier than on lakes closer to sea level.

You can park at km 22.4 (mi 13.9) and hike down to the earth dam at the reservoir's west end. Completed in 1912, the dam at Bear Creek Reservoir is about 18 m (60 ft) high. It is one of three reservoirs that provide water for B.C. Hydro's Jordan River power station. At one time you could cut left at km 23.8 (mi 14.8) onto the road between Bear Creek Reservoir and Diversion Reservoir and go all the way to Diversion Dam. The gate at this turnoff has been locked for some time now. Just down the road is another gate (km 24.5/mi 15.2) that for years was the end of the line for many backwoods browsers. Canadian Pacific Forest Products (CPFP) used to keep it locked after working hours, but now it is usually open. We seized the opportunity and spent a day exploring what was for us untravelled territory.

On the west side of the Jordan River bridge (km 25/mi 15.5) the road splits. Walker Main is to the left; Jordan Main on the right can be followed north to the Renfrew Road, near Floodwood Creek. We went left onto Walker Main. Almost immediately we cut onto a secondary road. This brought us to a bridge over Walker Creek. Most of the route ran through logged-off forest. Slash burning in the area was recent as evidenced by the sea of charred stumps on the mountainsides. About 5 km (3.1 mi) from the Walker/Jordan junction we were able to see Diversion Reservoir and its dam.

We negotiated a hairpin corner that looked about ready to cave in, what with the deep ditches on either side of the roadway. At a fork we cut down a hill, crossed the Wye Creek bridge and went east to Diversion Dam. On our way back to our Bear Creek Reservoir campsite we also explored the right-hand road at the fork. We didn't get too far due to an impassable washout. We kept going—on foot. We had lost sight of the dam by now, but the road snaked on to some lofty views of the Wye Creek Valley. It may be some time before we travel these arteries again. One of the bridges en route has since been swept away by a flooded creek.

CPFP informs me that they frequently haul down Walker Main and Jordan Main, east to Shawnigan Lake. Some hauling is also taking place near Williams Creek. The company has maintained an open-gate policy for the last couple of years, although active logging areas are still gated after hours. Some Island adventurers know the Sooke Hills so well that they rarely consult their maps. But the maps don't tell you everything. Conditions on the backroads are always changing. This chameleon-like nature of logging roads lures many visitors back.

Contacts

Canadian Pacific Forest Products (Cowichan Division) (604) 749-3796; Canadian Pacific Forest Products (Ladysmith) (604) 245-3233; B.C. Forest Service (Duncan) (604) 746-2700.

Maps/Guides

Guide to the Forestland of Southern Vancouver Island (LCCFO); National Topographical Series: 92B/5 Sooke (1:50,000); 92B/12 Shawnigan Lake (1:50,000); Provincial Map: 92B/NW Victoria (1:125,000).

Nearest Services

Sooke.

TRIP 5: Shawnigan Division Backroads

In Brief

MacMillan Bloedel's (Mac/Blo) Shawnigan Division, southwest of Duncan, has oodles of backroads and several lakes known for their spring and fall fishing. Pockets of old growth and viewpoints are other highlights. Some lakes have primitive, user-maintained campsites on their shores.

Access

Take the Bright Angel Park turn on Highway 1 and follow Koksilah, Miller and Glenora roads to the Deerholme gate. (You can also reach Glenora Road via Allenby and Indian roads.) Mainlines are in good-to fair-shape, with some steep hills; secondary roads air fair and could require a 4 x 4. Public access is permitted only on weekends and holidays (between 6:00 a.m. and 6:00 p.m.).

Description

One of the hardest things about MacMillan Bloedel's Shawnigan Division isn't the confusion or condition of the roads; most area mainlines are clearly signposted and in good shape. The problem is locating the start of this backroads jaunt in the Deerholme/Glenora district, southwest of Duncan.

You can wind your way there by taking the Bright Angel Park turn off Highway 1 and following Koksilah Road, Miller Road and then Glenora Road to the Shawnigan Division's main gate in Deerholme.

Breaking through the reeds at Lois Lake.

This route is about 13 km (8 mi) in length. You can also take Allenby and Indian roads to the Glenora Road entrance. Travelling through Mac/Blo's main gate is the only public access to the region, and even that is restricted to weekends and holidays only (between 6:00 a.m. and 6:00 p.m.). The watchman stationed there will normally ask your destination and length of stay. Similar security procedures are used at Fletcher Challenge's Nanaimo Lakes area. You can usually obtain a photocopy of the region's logging roads at the gate. Remember to reset your vehicle's trip meter to zero as you enter the Shawnigan Division.

At km 0.3 (mi 0.2) cut right onto the logging-yard bypass road. This stretch is usually bumpy and runs alongside an old railway track bed. At km 4.3 (mi 2.7) you'll reach the Keating Lake turn. There is a picnic site at Keating Lake and anglers will find good cutthroat trout action in the spring. It helps to have a belly boat, small cartopper or canoe so you can get out from the lake's marshy fringes into deeper water.

Right after the Keating Lake turn, Branch H200 angles off on the left (km 4.4/mi 2.7). You can follow this secondary road to Lois Lake along a series of backroads that climb up to Koksilah Ridge. There are many unmarked intersections, so it's easy to become lost. You can also work your way in to Lois Lake from a spur just north of Wild Deer Lake.

MacMillan Bloedel's Wild
Deer Lake Recreation Area is
a popular weekend destination.

The mainline climbs a long, steep hill in the Holt Creek Valley. At km 9.6 (mi 6) the road forks. U Line keeps straight ahead. H, L and W lines and Wild Deer Lake are to the left. Let's take a quick run in to Wild Deer Lake. Keep left onto H Line at km 10.5 (mi 6.5). Straight ahead is known as the Crossover, a bypass that loops back around to U Line. The road splits again at km 12 (mi 7.5). The left spur here is an alternate route to Lois Lake.

On one trip a friend and I attempted to find Lois Lake via this spur, just north of Wild Deer Lake. We brought out our maps and set off. We wound our way up the mountainside, encountered countless side roads and confusing intersections to somehow end up on the south side of Lois Lake. At the lake's north end a weathered wooden boardwalk and trail run to the water's edge. Like Keating Lake, Lois Lake requires a belly boat, cartopper or canoe to fish properly. Canoeists and boaters must glide through yielding reeds that stick up from shallow, shoreline waters. Current regulations restrict anglers to one fish a day and you may only use artificial flies.

You can continue on and hook into the steep switchback east of Glenora Creek to connect with L Line and Branch H200, near the Keating Lake access. On the way down you'll be treated to several panoramic views of the Cowichan Valley, Mount Prevost and Duncan.

Keep right at the 12-km (7.5-mi) junction onto W Line. You'll hit a second major fork at km 13.6 (mi 8.4). Keep left to stay on W Line. Wild Deer Lake will soon be visible on the right. Watch for the entrance to Mac/Blo's Wild Deer Lake Recreation Area (km 15/mi 9.3). Visitors will find primitive campsites, a natural boat launch, a wharf and a gravel beach area. There are no comfort stations. Wild Deer Lake is a popular fly-casting destination for May anglers. The lake holds cutthroat and rainbow trout and in recent years has been stocked with rainbow yearlings. No powerboats are allowed on the lake.

On one backroads adventure in the Shawnigan Division I stayed on U Line at the km-9.6 (mi-6) junction. The road climbs a grade to meet the Crossover loop (km 10.9/mi 6.8) and veers to the right. At km 15.7 (mi 9.7) I swung left over a bridge onto M Line; straight ahead was S Main. F Line (km 18.7/mi 11.6) intersects M Line on the right. Some backwoods browsers take this artery and wind around the north side of Waterloo Mountain. At km 22 (mi 13.7), X Line meets M Line. I headed west on X Line to a secondary spur along which is an impressive stand of old-growth forest. Much of the Shawnigan Division displays the marks of logging, but the old growth near Waterloo Mountain is one exception. If you have a 4 x 4, you can take some of the spur roads to high-elevation viewpoints of the surrounding area.

There are several other lakes in the region: Pete's Pond and Long Lake (both accessed from side roads along S Main), and Tadjiss (Crescent) Lake on C Main. There are even some unnamed ponds and widenings of the creeks and rivers. You'll find primitive campsites near Pete's Pond and Long Lake. The same restrictions that apply for Lois Lake are in place on Tadjiss Lake. You can't keep any trout on Pete's Pond, but that won't keep all anglers away; those already practising catch-and-release will find this tiny, high-elevation lake a treat. As you become more familiar with the alphabetically named backroads to these elusive Shawnigan Division fishing spots, finding your way will be as easy as A-B-C.

Contacts

MacMillan Bloedel (Cowichan Division) (604) 246-4714; B.C. Forest Service (Duncan) (604) 746-2700.

Maps/Guides

MacMillan Bloedel Cowichan Division Recreation and Logging Road Guide; Guide to the Forestland of Southern Vancouver Island (LCCFO); National Topographical Series: 92B/12 Shawnigan Lake (1:50,000); 92B/13 Duncan (1:50,000); Provincial Map: 92B/NW Victoria (1:125,000).

Nearest Services

Duncan area.

TRIP 6: The Kinsol Trestle

In Brief

The highest and longest known wooden railway trestle in Canada spans a deep gorge of the Koksilah River, northwest of Shawnigan Lake. The span is 44.2 m (145 ft) high and 187.2 m (614 ft) long. The bridge is now in disrepair, and access is limited, but a visit to this historic point of interest is worth the effort.

Access

From the north: take the Bright Angel Park turn, on Highway 1, drive through Cowichan Station to Riverside Road and continue about 10 km (6.2 mi) to the railway right-of-way. From the south: follow Renfrew Road, west of Shawnigan Lake, to Gleneagle Road. Turn right and travel about 1 km (0.6 mi) to the railway right-of-way. Parking is limited at the access points. Visitors should respect private property in the area. Parts of the routes are gravel.

Description

When I was younger, I was fascinated by trains, rail lines and train bridges. Almost daily after school I would bike to a CPR mainline to catch the passing of a passenger or freight train. Sometimes I would get a wave from an engineer or the railman in a caboose. Forbidden walks on lofty rail bridges and trestles highlighted my forays. My boyhood passion was rekindled years ago when I first heard tell of the

Kinsol Trestle, an immense wooden rail bridge spanning the Koksilah River. Since then I have visited the trestle many times.

There are two approaches to the trestle site. From Highway 1 take the South Shawnigan Lake turn or the Mill Bay cutoff and travel around the north end of Shawnigan Lake to the Renfrew Road. From the junction of West Shawnigan Lake Road and Renfrew Road it's about 2 km (1.2 mi) to Gleneagle Road. Turn right and continue about 1 km (0.6 mi) to the railway right-of-way. Parking is limited here and visitors must respect private property. You can walk along the right-of-way to the trestle.

The best perspective of the old bridge is from the north side of the Koksilah River. Take the signposted Bright Angel Park turn on Highway 1, and stay on Koksilah Road to Cowichan Station. Travel under the narrow E & N Railway overpass, cross the Koksilah River bridge to Riverside Road (km 2.3/mi 1.4). Turn left and continue about 9.5 km (5.9 mi) to the railway right-of-way. There are a couple of views over to Saltspring Island en route. As with the southern access, parking is scarce and when you locate the right-of-way you have to walk the final 0.5 km (0.3 mi) or so to the trestle on foot.

Canadian Northern Pacific initiated work on a rail line in 1911. Progress was slow due to the company's debts and the outbreak of World War I. Timber cut for the trestle's construction was piled on both sides of the Koksilah River, but this rotted before it was used. The federal government acquired the line, and bridge work was completed by the CNR in 1920. The name is short for King Solomon, named after the Kinsol copper mine that operated in the area in the early 1900s. Over the next four decades a number of sawmills existed in the region, all of which were destroyed by fire. Over the winter of 1930-31 heavy rains flooded the Koksilah River. Branches, debris and even whole trees were swept down the swollen river, causing extensive damage to the trestle. Intermittent repair work was started and by 1936, the bridge's superstructure had been rebuilt on six Howe trusses and huge concrete piers. Further reconditioning took place in 1958 and 1973-74 with the replacement of rotting timbers and trestle-support structures (bents). The rail line was instrumental in the opening up of the Cowichan Valley's early forest industry. The bridge was used primarily by the logging industry to bring in equipment and supplies and to carry Cowichan Lake timber to Victoria mills. Scheduled gas-car runs were prevalent in the 1920s; in the fall of 1958 a CNR museum train, carrying passengers, negotiated the span as part of a south-Island tour. The last train went

The Kinsol Trestle spans a deep gorge of the Koksilah River.

across in 1979, with a four-car load of cedar poles. The line was abandoned in 1980.

Since that time there has been recurring talk of restoring the bridge and making the area a historic viewing site. The most recent attempt was in 1992. There are a number of concerns. Some local residents are against this plan; they feel their privacy would be at risk. Both access routes to the site are barricaded by boulders and there is limited parking. Incidents of vandalism have occurred in the past; in 1977, there was a death at the site, and in 1988, a campfire foolishly started on the trestle got out of control. The Island gas line crosses the Koksilah River close by. The two biggest stumbling blocks are the high cost of restorations and maintenance and the liabilities for public safety.

The opportunity to preserve the Kinsol Trestle in its beautiful setting still exists, though some estimates show that without expedient attention, the structure could collapse within two decades—and that would be a shame.

Contacts

Ecomuseum (Duncan) (604) 746-1611; B.C. Forest Service (Duncan) (604) 746-2700.

Maps/Guides

Guide to the Forestland of Southern Vancouver Island (LCCFO); National Topographical Series: 92B/12 Shawnigan Lake (1:50,000); Provincial Map: 92B/NW Victoria (1:125,000).

Nearest Services

Shawnigan Lake; Cowichan Station.

TRIP 7: Port Renfrew to Cowichan Lake

In Brief

Taking Gordon River Main from Port Renfrew to Cowichan Lake appeals to many Island adventurers. Travellers with four-wheelers can explore area backroads to several vistas. Grant's Grove, a pocket stand of old growth, is on the way, as is the trail to the heights of Mount Sutton. You can hook up with Cowichan Lake's South Shore Road at either Honeymoon Bay or just east of Caycuse.

Access

Follow the West Coast Road (Highway 14) to Port Renfrew. Cross the white bridge spanning the San Juan River to the Deering Bridge over the river's north branch. Turn left and travel about 1 km (0.6 mi) to the entrance to the Port Renfrew marina. Gravel mainlines are in good-to-fair shape; secondary roads may require a high-slung vehicle or 4 x 4. Active hauling may be encountered on the mainlines. At such times Fletcher Challenge recommends travelling after weekday working hours.

Description

Many backwoods browsers are familiar with the backroads from the Port Renfrew area, up the Harris Creek Valley to Mesachie Lake, on Cowichan Lake. You can also take Fletcher Challenge's Gordon Main. The starting point for this alternate route is the entrance to the Port

A neglected trestle near the Deering Bridge over the San Juan River.

Renfrew marina, about 1 km (0.6 mi) west of the Deering Bridge. Take Highway 14 to Port Renfrew and follow the marina/West Coast Trail signposts. Cross the white bridge over the San Juan River to the Deering Bridge, which spans the north branch of the river. (*Island Adventures*: Trip 1.) At the T-junction turn left and travel about 1 km (0.6 mi) to the marina entrance and reset your vehicle's trip meter to zero.

The Port Renfrew marina has been in operation since 1988, near the site of a former logging camp. The marina caters to thousands of saltwater anglers annually. Facilities include RV and tent campsites, comfort stations, well water and a sani-station. Electric power is not available. There is a concrete boat ramp and ample moorage.

Port Renfrew waters offer excellent bottom fishing—halibut are plentiful—and there is good crabbing. All species of salmon are present. Mooching for chinooks in the West Point (Owen Point) area is popular from early July to late August. Anglers with boats capable of tackling the sometimes rough seas near Carmanah Point will find good coho fishing in that vicinity. Zero tides are a problem at the shallow mouth of the Gordon River. Boaters usually negotiate this spot at tides of 0.5 m (1.6 ft) or higher. Mornings are generally quiet on Port San Juan, though fog frequently rolls in. By late afternoon prevailing westerlies are up.

From the marina entrance the mainline crosses Browns Creek and follows the Gordon River to the bridge (km 4.2/mi 2.6). Braden Main goes straight ahead. You can explore Braden Main to parallel Braden Creek and run along the east side of Edinburgh Mountain before rejoining Gordon Main. Swing left to stay on Gordon River Main and cross the bridge. You might be inclined to park on either side of the bridge (make sure you're well off to the shoulder of the road) for an extended look at the river.

Big-lake paddlers can usually avoid the daily waves by travelling in the early morning.

Make a right on the west side of the bridge. Straight ahead is Grierson Main and the junction with Pandora Main. Both Grierson and Pandora mainlines lead to commanding viewpoints of the surrounding mountains and Port San Juan. Most of the views are along spur roads, which often require a high-slung truck or 4 x 4. Fletcher Challenge has been hauling down Grierson Main and Gordon River Main. During periods of heavy industrial traffic, the company suggests visitors time their travels to after weekday working hours or on weekends and holidays.

Gordon River Main closely follows the river. To the east the view is dominated by Edinburgh Mountain. At km 11.7 (mi 7.3) Bugaboo Main swings off to the left to follow the banks of Bugaboo Creek. Near Loup Creek, Branch 4000 can be followed to a trail through a pocket stand of old growth, known as Grant's Grove. Several huge Douglas fir and western red cedar trees can be sought out by backwoods browsers.

At km 18.6 (mi 11.6) Braden Main hooks back into Gordon River Main. Our route continues up the Gordon River Valley, with Mount Walbran to the west; Mount Bolduc to the east. An old trestle, around the 26.5-km (16.5-mi) mark, is one stop of interest. At km 30.2 (mi 18.8) the road cuts through the Fletcher Challenge Gordon River Camp. In 1992, the logging company shut down operations at Caycuse and shifted them over to the Gordon River site.

There's a major junction at km 34.6 (mi 21.5). Swing left onto the

Renfrew Hookup, which heads north to make a serpentine descent onto Cowichan Lake's South Shore Road, just east of Caycuse. At this point (km 45.7/mi 28.4) you can turn left for the head of Cowichan Lake and Nitinat Main or cut right for Honeymoon Bay. You can also keep right at the 34.6-km (21.5-mi) mark and journey down the mainline alongside Sutton Creek to eventually meet the South Shore Road near the wildflower reserve or closer to Honeymoon Bay.

Just south of the Renfrew Hookup turn is the trailhead used by hikers tackling the trail up Mount Sutton, the mountain directly north of Gordon River Camp. There is plenty of room to park a vehicle where the mainline widens next to a stand of alders. Highlights of the first part of the hike are the cable car across the Gordon River and the box canyon to the north. More adventurous hikers will continue up the steep path—more of a route in some sections—to Mount Sutton's summit. It's best to travel with someone who knows the area, as it's easy to become lost.

Contacts

Fletcher Challenge (Honeymoon Bay) (604) 749-6805; B.C. Forest Service (Duncan) 746-2700.

Maps/Guides

Guide to the Forestland of Southern Vancouver Island (LCCFO); B.C. Forest Service Duncan Forest District Recreation Map; Hiking Trails II (Outdoor Club of Victoria Trails Information Society); National Topographical Series: 92C/9 Port Renfrew (1:50,000); 92C/16 Lake Cowichan (1:50,000); Provincial Map: 92C/NE Nitinat Lake (1:125,000).

Nearest Services

Port Renfrew; Lake Cowichan area.

TRIP 8: Journey to the Walbran Valley

In Brief

An exceptional wilderness hiking destination on southern Vancouver Island is the Walbran Valley. Rugged trails lead through an ancient forest of cedar, hemlock and fir to pristine lakes, river canyons and waterfalls.

Access

From the village of Lake Cowichan, west of Duncan, take the South Shore Road through Honeymoon Bay to Caycuse. Cross the Nixon Creek bridge. (*Island Adventures*: Trip 9.) South Shore Road swings right; keep straight ahead on Caycuse (Nixon Creek) Main for the Walbran. Gravel mainlines are in good-to-fair shape. Sharp rocks, gravel ridges and rougher sections may be encountered. There is active hauling on some area mainlines. It's best to travel on these arteries after 6:00 p.m. on weekdays.

Description

The start of the run to the Walbran Valley is along Cowichan Lake's South Shore Road. Frequent backwoods browsers are already familiar with the new section of the South Shore Road, opened in 1990. It begins soon after you hit the gravel near the Honeymoon Bay Wildflower Reserve. The new route bypasses a steep grade in the Millar Creek Valley. Island adventurers now follow a course along the ridges closer to the lake.

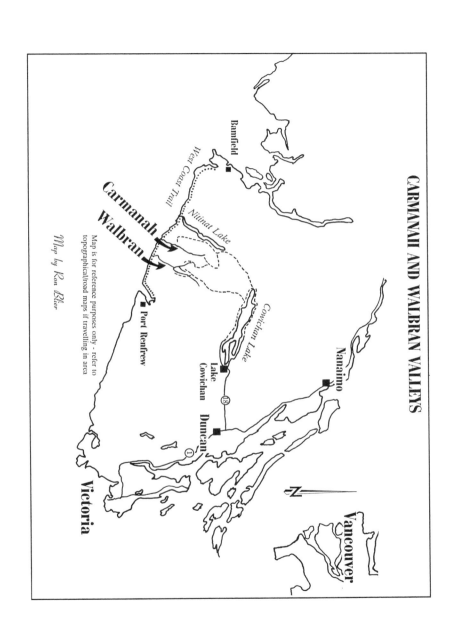

CARMANAH AND WALBRAN VALLEYS

Bamfield

West Coast Trail

Nitinat Lake

Carmanah
Walbran

Cowichan Lake

Port Renfrew

Map is for reference purposes only - refer to
topographical/road maps if travelling in area

Map by Ron Bluer

Lake
Cowichan

18

Duncan

Nanaimo

1

N

Victoria

Vancouver

The road was built to avoid a hairpin corner and lengthy hill that, over the years, unnerved countless first-time travellers. The route taxed many a vehicle, whether they were labouring up or slipping down the long incline. Two successive grades, totalling over 1.5 km (0.9 mi) in length had also been a problem for logging trucks. The heavily laden vehicles were slow-going as they inched up the challenging slope. Negotiating the hill was hard on mechanical parts. Frost on the roadway was prevalent in the winter and the route traversed a region frequently above the snow line. One Fletcher Challenge employee likened a loaded logging truck in icy conditions to a big toboggan. He explained that with increased hauling out of the neighbouring valleys, relocating part of the South Shore Road was essential. The new road adds 1.1 km (0.7 mi) to a jaunt along Cowichan Lake's south side. One highlight is a riveting viewpoint of the lake and the craggy rock faces of Bald Mountain.

Hunters and other outdoorsmen can still access area spur roads they've come to know; their only obstacle will be whatever toll Mother Nature exacts on the redundant stretch of backroad. The old route receives little maintenance. After only a couple of years of non-use, erosion is evident, especially near the hairpin corner. Undetectable sinkholes sometimes undermine portions of the roadway.

South Shore Road runs by Caycuse and heads west. In 1992, Fletcher Challenge closed down the camp and moved to Gordon River, closer to Port Renfrew. (See Trip 7.) Cross the Nixon Creek bridge and keep straight ahead on Nixon Creek (Caycuse) Main. Don't forget to reset your vehicle's trip meter. In the first stretch there are patches of old pavement put down in the 1960s. The forest here is predominantly alder and maple. The Walbran Valley consists of cedar, hemlock and fir, with some patchy spruce growth. You'll cross two bridges and then the road starts to climb a long, steep hill to the Caycuse Summit, near the 486-m (1600-ft) level. Heavy snowfall over the winter months sometimes plugs the route. Residual snows can often be seen in shady pockets well into May; sometimes even June. The grade is bumpy in spots with rocky sections. This region was once rail-logged and the mainline follows the same switchbacks as the railway did. With the advent of truck logging in the 1950s, roads soon replaced the rail lines.

At km 8.1 (mi 5) keep left. Side roads are many, but they are obviously spurs. One artery leads over to Nitinat Lake, a rough but passable route. Rocky outcrops are prevalent close to the road. At km 10.5 (mi 6.5) you will reach the junction with McLure Lake Main.

The Caycuse Fir is one point of interest on the backroad to the lower Walbran Valley.

Swing left at this point. On one trip we saw a mountain biker on his way out. The route is passable in a regular passenger vehicle, but you have to drive at a snail's pace where the road is rough.

Bald mountaintops become visible at km 11.8 (mi 7.3), followed by a stunning view of an old-growth valley (km 13.5/mi 8.4). The mainline continues through clearcuts to the branch road for the Caycuse Fir (km 14.9/mi 9.3). The access spur is driveable to the signposted trail to the ancient tree, 0.6 km (0.4 mi) from the mainline. Though its top has long since toppled off, the 1200-year-old Douglas fir still guards over a second-growth forest. An excellent perspective of the tree is on the mainline, a little beyond the access spur. Here, at a switchback and bridge, the road skirts behind the ridge on which the aging forest veteran stands. Some wolf trapping has occurred in the region and the area is prime deer wintering range.

Bridge improvements and culvert replacements have taken place in the next stretch. At km 22.6 (mi 14) McLure Lake will be visible on the left. Watch for a short side road to lakeside that goes to a couple of wilderness campsites. The road skirts McLure Lake and a pond further west to a gate and watchman's post at km 26.2 (mi 16.3). At a key junction (km 26.4/mi 16.4) go left onto Glad Lake Main. The route roughens somewhat to run through clearcuts interspersed with stands of old-growth forest. The Walbran Creek bridge is at km 29.1 (mi 18.1). Logging in this region has gone right down to the creekside. Some of the trees left standing near the creek have toppled since the loggers have moved on.

By km 35.5 (mi 22) the old-growth forest dominates. Gravel ridges and rocks will slow down your pace. You'll traverse a potential rock-slide area with the deep river valley to the right. Then comes a hill and more switchbacks. At km 38.4 (mi 23.8) is the South Walbran Creek bridge. Keep left at km 39.9 (mi 24.8); to the right is branch GL18. For a while the roadway improves. Another viewpoint looking over an old-growth valley is on the right at km 40.4 (mi 25.1). At the Glad Lake West junction (km 41.6/mi 25.8) keep right. The spur roads in this vicinity look very much like the mainline, so it can be confusing. When Fletcher Challenge carved their access roads in, the company used as much of the blasted rock as possible during road construction. Costs per km (0.6 mi) were between $60,000 and $70,000. Keep left at km 42.5 (mi 26.4). Branch GL50 cuts to the right. Just over the 43-km (26.7-mi) mark you'll reach the Walbran Creek bridge. The lower Walbran trailhead starts on the far side.

Annual rainfall increases dramatically the closer you are to the Island's west coast. Duncan averages 890 mm (35 in); Lake Cowichan 1524 mm (60 in); and Caycuse 2540 mm (100 in). The Walbran, on the west side of Caycuse Summit, averages a whopping 5080 mm (200 in)! If you hike unprepared in the Walbran Valley and get caught by one of its typically deluging rainfalls, you are going to become very, very wet. Always carry adequate rainwear on extended journeys.

Since my first visit to the lower Walbran Valley a few years ago (on a Fletcher Challenge forestry tour), the first part of the trail has been improved a little. A cedar-plank boardwalk is in place most of the way to the side path to lower Fletcher Falls, on West Walbran Creek. Wear hiking boots and take care during damp or wet weather; it can still be slippery going. Not all the muddy areas are covered by boardwalk. The rough stairs on the steep bank to the upper falls area were under repair the last time I hiked in. When the water in West Walbran Creek is low enough, you can walk out on the rocks for a closer look at the falls.

Signs erected by B.C. Environment inform anglers of the trout and kokanee release regulations in place on West Walbran Creek. Only artificial flies may be used on the stream. A cable car crosses the creek just east of the falls. Cedars in this vicinity are of immense girth and over 1000 years old. Soon you will pass the steeper sections of the trail and find relatively easy going along the valley floor. There are still some tricky creek crossings ahead, notable at Botley

Creek and the one just before the Fetus Lake trail junction. It is easy to lose the route in some places, so be alert. Look for flagged branches. Maxine's Tree, the biggest Sitka spruce yet found in the Walbran Valley, is northeast of Fetus Lake. It ranks among Canada's largest trees.

You can hike to Anderson Lake and continue all the way to West Walbran trailhead. To reach this Walbran Valley access, take the backroads for the Carmanah Valley to the Caycuse River bridge. (See Trip 9.) Cut left onto South Main (Carmanah Main on older maps) for Haddon Main; then take Mac/Blo's Roane Main to Branch H1000. The trailhead is about 20 km (12.4 mi) from the Caycuse River bridge. Some travellers park at one trailhead and start their hiking at the other by driving there in a second vehicle.

As of this writing, fall 1992, the fate of the lower Walbran Valley remains uncertain. A temporary log-around plan, implemented by the NDP government under the Old Growth Strategy program, expires in mid-1993. In the meantime both Fletcher Challenge and MacMillan Bloedel will continue harvesting selected cutblocks in the upper valley. For many, extensive logging is already dangerously close to the relatively untouched lower Walbran. Only if protected status comes to the area soon will future generations be able to sample its wilderness atmosphere.

Contacts

Fletcher Challenge (Honeymoon Bay) (604) 749-6805; MacMillan Bloedel (Cameron/Franklin Division) (604) 723-9471; B.C. Forest Service (Duncan) (604) 746-2700; Western Canada Wilderness Committee (Victoria) (604) 388-9292.

Maps/Guides

Western Canada Wilderness Committee Walbran guide; MacMillan Bloedel TFL 44 Recreation and Logging Road Guide (East Map); Guide to the Forestland of Southern Vancouver Island (LCCFO); B.C. Forest Service Duncan Forest District Recreation Map; National Topographical Series: 92C/10 Carmanah Creek (1:50,000); 92C/15 Little Nitinat River (1:50,000); 92C/16 Cowichan Lake (1:50,000); Provincial Map: Regional Map #2 Parksville/Tofino (1:125,000).

Nearest Services

Lake Cowichan area.

TRIP 9: Backroads to the Carmanah Valley

In Brief

Carmanah Pacific Provincial Park, created in June 1990, attracts countless visitors to the giant spruce groves in the Carmanah Valley. And getting there is half the adventure.

Access

From the Nitinat Junction near the top end of Nitinat Lake (*Island Adventures*: Trip 10) follow the mainlines to the park trailheads. The route is in good-to-fair shape, with several steep grades. Industrial traffic may be frequent in some sections. Secondary spur explorations may require a 4 x 4.

Description

Different people return with disparate impressions after venturing on the backroads to the Carmanah Valley. Those who travel Island logging roads infrequently may consider the region remote—the roads gruelling. Habitual backwoods browsers will have more tempered opinions. My initial taste of the Nitinat came in the 1970s, from the waters of Nitinat Lake. At that time my brother and I embarked on the first of what would be many paddling forays down the lake to its lower reaches near the Nitinat Narrows.

On our earliest trip, as we approached Daykins Bay, we heard the drone of a generator somewhere up ahead. The low humming, it was soon discovered, came from an active Malloch and Moseley logging camp on the shore. During a lunch break on the rocky islet in Daykins Bay we noticed a logging road that ran through the camp, parallelled the cove, and then disappeared over a rise near a recent cutblock. We saw a fair amount of traffic on the gravel artery and became convinced there must be a road link not indicated on the logging company maps and various other charts we referred to while plotting our trip. Subsequent investigation revealed there was indeed a land route to the now-dismantled logging camp, and on our very next backroads outing, it was the one we took. Back then the farthest you could go on the combined-use logging roads was the Caycuse Creek bridge. There you encountered active logging areas with restricted access.

On one trip we reached Caycuse Creek way ahead of our planned schedule. That meant an hour's wait until 5:00 p.m. rolled around. By then the logging activities would cease for the day and most of the hauling—by the big off-road behemoths—would be over. We'd seen our share of trucks on the stretch of mainline running west from the Nitinat River bridge to Caycuse Creek. Some of the felled timber coming out was so huge that only one or two giant logs could be carried by the haulers.

A logging company pickup suddenly appeared over a rise, decelerated and turned to cross the bridge. The driver slowed as he went by and I threw out a quick question on current access. "You're okay now," he replied. "There's only one or two more trucks on their way out. When they go by, you can head on in." Maybe we weren't too much ahead of schedule after all.

Today this same mainline is travelled by countless Island adventurers on their way to Carmanah Pacific Provincial Park and its stands of giant spruce. Parts of the route are now much wider and roadside clearing has eliminated some blind corners. You may still encounter slight delays on weekdays. Follow any instructions given to travellers at logging checkpoints. And if you don't relish tangling with a loaded truck on your way in, simply plan to tackle the hauling roads after the weekday logging crews have shut down (usually by 6:00 p.m.) or on weekends. Don't forget to gas up in the Lake Cowichan area; there are no services once you hit the logging roads.

First, take one of the well-travelled mainlines around Cowichan Lake and head west. In 1990, a new section of the South Shore Road was opened to bypass a couple of long, steep hills and a switchback. The new route adds 1.1 km (0.7 mi) to a run along Cowichan Lake's

Rosander Main climbs a steep switchback to a stunning vista of Nitinat Lake's top end.

south side. The mainlines converge at the lakehead near the Heather Campsite boat launch. The logging road leading to the Nitinat Valley meets the Cowichan Lake roads at a signposted junction. Reset your vehicle's trip meter to zero at this point and cut west onto Nitinat Main.

Backwoods browsers will find many disused railway trestles on Island backroads. The weathered bridge at Vernon Creek is one such relic from the days of rail-logging. It was built in 1933 by Industrial Timber Mills of Youbou. The route to Carmanah Valley splits into a one-way section for a while and then parallels the Nitinat River. Mac-Millan Bloedel (Mac/Blo) has established a primitive riverside picnic site (km 18.3/mi 11.4). Watch for the entrance on the right. The look of this spot changes each year and it's intriguing to see just what alterations the Nitinat River has imposed on the site following winter high water. Just ahead you'll reach what is known as the Nitinat Junction (km 18.5/mi 11.5). Port Alberni and Bamfield travellers keep right at this intersection and cross the Nitinat River bridge. It's about 62.5 km (39 mi) from here to Port Alberni. Island adventurers heading to the Carmanah Valley will bear left onto South Main (Carmanah Main on older maps).

At the Nitinat Junction again reset your trip meter to zero and bear left. The mainline crosses Campus Creek (km 4.4/mi 2.7). Keep left at the next fork (km 5.5/mi 3.4) and climb the hill. The secondary road for Mac/Blo's Nitinat campsite is on the right at km 7.8 (mi 4.8). It's a short distance from the mainline to the campsite entrance. Many Carmanah Valley visitors base camp here and daytrip to the area's hiking trails. Mac/Blo has been promoting this user-maintained facility as a windsurfing hot spot, and it's easy to see why. Daily winds out on Nitinat Lake provide exhilarating sport for sailboarders. The campsites are within a stand of old-growth forest, through which a trail curves down to the mouth of Caycuse Creek. You can return to camp along Nitinat Lake's shoreline. The area's greater popularity makes it harder, at times, to find a vacant site at the top end of Nitinat Lake. Conditions on long weekends are notoriously crowded. Backwoods browsers who have used this locale for decades can still savour the sense of wilderness magic and solitude that exists in the Nitinat Valley. It's just a matter of coinciding your backroad forays with the off-season.

Beyond the campsite turnoff, South Main swings east into the lower Caycuse Creek Valley. At km 9.1 (mi 5.7) you'll reach the Caycuse River bridge. On the far side is a T-junction. A left here follows South Main to active logging regions northeast of Mount Walbran. Hikers can access the Walbran Valley by taking South, Haddon and Roane mainlines and a branch road to the West Walbran trailhead. (See Trip 8.) Turn right at the Caycuse bridge onto Rosander Main for Carmanah Pacific Provincial Park.

Soon after you cut onto Rosander Main the road crosses Hooper Creek. You might want to stop and take a look at the precipitous limestone canyon that Hooper Creek has carved out over the centuries. Make sure to park your vehicle well off on the shoulder of the mainline. Rosander Main curves back towards Nitinat Lake. Logging cutblocks in this region have opened up the forest and you'll be able to see Nitinat Lake at several points. I've been fortunate enough to traverse this area prior to the clearcutting—when tall Douglas fir and cedar still lined the roadside.

The next stretch of the run to the Carmanah Valley is my favourite part, although on the first trip through I wondered what I was getting myself into. At km 14.6 (mi 9.1) a steep, seemingly unending grade begins. The mainline hugs the northwest flank of Mount Rosander to a sharp switchback; then it's uphill once again. Just under the 16-km (9.9-mi) mark is a stunning vista over Caycuse Creek and the top end of Nitinat Lake.

The road levels off and runs through a narrow pass. Just beyond

Rosander Main snakes through a pass near Rosander Lake.

Rosander Lake there is an old spur (on the left) that splits into a couple of washed-out roads leading up a west slope of Mount Rosander. Several commanding viewpoints can be found along these arteries—one looks west, down Nitinat Lake to the Pacific Ocean. Last time I was on these backroads they were passable in a high-slung 4 x 4; there were a few deteriorating washouts that are probably even rougher now. If you're travelling in a normal passenger vehicle, it's best to park at the base of the hills and hike up.

Rosander Main passes a small roadside lake and then crosses a bridge before plunging into the Marchand Creek drainage. There are a few blind corners in this vicinity. Drive with caution on the bridge approaches, while negotiating switchbacks and near steep sandbanks—particularly if you're driving a large vehicle or carrying a camper unit.

There is a plethora of potentially confusing (or intriguing, depending on your mood) side roads, junctions and intersections in the next part of the route. Ignore these spurs and keep straight ahead on Rosander Main. An exception might be the turnoff on the right, at km 24.7 (mi 15.3). From here you can hook up with the road that skirts the east side of Doobah Lake and dead-ends at the edge of a clearcut—the boundary of Pacific Rim National Park. The park's largest known western red cedars grow nearby, mainly on the east side of Cheewhat Lake. The Doobah Lake Cedar, on that lake's northern fringe, is another stop of interest. Randy Stoltmann's *Hiking Guide to the Big Trees of Southwestern British Columbia* contains a section on the Cheewhat area and its tree-viewing potential. A rugged trail wends to the lake, and some people I've talked with have portaged canoes in.

One paddler attempted to journey from Cheewhat Lake down the Cheewhat River, in hopes of reaching the West Coast Trail. He didn't get too far; fallen trees and a tangle of underbrush changed his mind rather quickly.

Rosander Main runs south through a series of clearcuts separated by blocks of old-growth forest. The junction with Bonilla Main is at km 35 (mi 21.7). From here the road swings east to the parking lot and main trailhead (km 37.6/mi 23.3). Prior to the creation of Carmanah Pacific Provincial Park in June 1990, visitors could access an alternate trail along a spur road off Bonilla Main. Today a locked gate bars entry to Bonilla Main.

From the parking lot the trail leads visitors into the magnificent old-growth forest along Carmanah Creek. Trip 10 describes a hiking adventure in the Carmanah Valley.

Contacts

MacMillan Bloedel (Cameron/Franklin Division) (604) 723-9471; B.C. Forest Service (Port Alberni) (604) 724-9205; B.C. Parks (Malahat District) (604) 387-4363; B.C. Parks (Victoria) (604) 387-5002; B.C. Parks Public Information Officer (Victoria) (604) 387-4609; Western Canada Wilderness Committee (Victoria) (604) 388-9292.

Maps/Guides

MacMillan Bloedel TFL 44 Recreation and Logging Road Guide (East Map); Western Canada Wilderness Committee Carmanah guide; Guide to the Forestland of Southern Vancouver Island (LCCFO); Parks Branch Carmanah Pacific Provincial Park brochure; B.C. Forest Service Port Alberni Forest District Recreation Map; *Hiking Guide to the Big Trees of Southwestern British Columbia* (Stoltmann/WCWC); National Topographical Series: 92C/10 Carmanah Creek (1:50,000); 92C/14 Barkley Sound (1:50,000); Provincial Map: Regional Map #2 Parksville/Tofino (1:125,000).

Nearest Services

Lake Cowichan area; Port Alberni.

TRIP 10: Hiking in the Carmanah Valley

In Brief

The creation of Carmanah Pacific Provincial Park in 1990 ensured preservation of an exceptional old-growth forest on Vancouver Island's west coast. Trails wind along Carmanah Creek to groves of ancient trees and beautiful river viewpoints. Many visitors day-hike from the parking lot; others tent at wilderness campsites along Carmanah Creek. A hike among the giant spruce in the Carmanah Valley is remembered long after you return to civilization.

Access

From Port Alberni or Lake Cowichan take the logging roads to the top end of Nitinat Lake. At the Nitinat Junction head west on South Main, then Rosander Main and follow the signs about 38 km (23.6 mi) to the park.

Description

The Carmanah Valley is home to the world's largest Sitka spruce trees. Valley slopes harbour twisted cedars, many over 1000 years old. Thriving in the damp environment close to the Pacific Ocean, scattered groves of towering spruce are accessed by trails snaking beneath a canopy of a diverse old-growth forest within Carmanah Pacific Provincial Park. In dry weather many park-goers camp at primitive campsites along Carmanah Creek.

The primitive trails in the lower Carmanah Valley are now closed to hikers.

Carmanah Pacific Provincial Park was created in June 1990, after years of bitter wrangling, bickering and cajoling by both those for and against Carmanah Valley's preservation. The extent of the park boundaries are a compromise that has neither side mollified. Maybe that's the mark of a good trade-off. The park is located at the end of MacMillan Bloedel's Rosander mainline. From the Nitinat Junction (on the Cowichan Lake/Port Alberni backroad, near Nitinat Lake's top end) it's just under 38 km (23.6 mi) to the trailhead. (See Trip 9.)

A year prior to the creation of Carmanah Pacific Provincial Park, two friends and I set off on a trek to the Carmanah Giant, Canada's tallest tree, located in the lower Carmanah Creek Valley. The trail we followed was a primitive track cut through by volunteer trail builders. MacMillan Bloedel was working along Rosander Main, so we had to use an alternate trailhead (since closed) on a spur road along Bonilla Main. A watchman at the logging checkpoint near the junction of Rosander and Bonilla mainlines gave us precise directions to this point.

From its start on Bonilla Main the route went downhill to join up with the existing trail from Rosander Main. The sound of chainsaws diminished as we wound down the switchbacks to river level. We went right at the Camp Heaven Junction towards the ford on Carmanah Creek. At the ford we got our feet a little wet; there was no avoiding it. One of my friends doffed his hiking boots and crossed the chilling stream barefoot.

The trails were primitive, with several log crossings. At some points we had to walk along mammoth deadfalls. Wire mesh had been placed on the fallen logs to provide some traction. Makeshift ropes had been set up as hand guides. We crossed numerous gulleys. Some of the steeper banks had crude steps cut into them. Switchbacks were many, and at a number of spots we had to hoist ourselves up the trail with the heavy hand ropes; with a full pack it was slow going. On a map the total distance from the ford to the Carmanah Giant was not that great, though it seemed much longer. The trail was rugged and the constant up-and-down going required concentrated attention.

We eventually reached the point where Bonilla Main was visible on the opposite side of the river. A couple of other travellers had set up a camp in their van at the end of the road. A highlight of the hike was Emerald Pool, a deep hole in Carmanah Creek where the water has scoured out an inviting swimming hole. The water in Carmanah Creek is very cold, even in the summer, but some people have braved the chill. By now we were tiring. We passed one possible camping spot, a tiny clearing in the forest. We pressed on to face yet another set of wooden ladders and eventually came to Mud Camp, a clearing near a small stream that had been used by trail builders as a base camp. Its name tells the story, but we did find some relatively dry ground to set up our tent.

From Mud Camp we day-hiked to the Carmanah Giant. We encountered the usual mudholes, creek crossings, fallen trees and rickety ladders. Silver Strand Falls was a delight to see. At one point we took a side trail, carved out of a massive deadfall, to arrive at a lofty viewpoint looking down into the Carmanah Creek canyon. The trail wound up to a plateau where we discovered easy hiking for a short distance. Then it was almost straight down to the creek via a sheer switchbacking route. Ropes were in place in the muddier sections and at the clay bank right at creekside.

We gazed up in awe at the Carmanah Giant, a towering spruce 95 m (312 ft) high. Estimated at less than 400 years of age, the tree is 3 m (10 ft) in diameter. It's hard to get a true perspective on the giant's size with the limited viewing available from the narrow creek bottom.

Slowly evening shadows crept over the forest. We gazed around us at the silent forest sentinels. The angled shapes of trees leaning or fallen over were harder to make out now with the coming of night's gloaming. It was easy to see why some Carmanah Valley visitors speak of its serenity and cathedral-like atmosphere. Later that night we heard owls hooting in the blackness. I attempted to imitate a call—surprisingly with some success—and we listened in amusement as one owl's calling got louder and louder. Our last contact came from directly behind our camp. The owl then realized its error and moved on.

Silver Strand Falls in the Carmanah Valley.

Visitors to Carmanah Pacific Provincial Park should expect slippery, muddy trails with some rough sections. Those planning on extended forays should be reasonably fit and familiar with wilderness travel. Gear up for primitive camping conditions. Carry raingear and warm clothing and expect changeable weather conditions. Strong, sturdy, water-resistant footwear is essential. Carry out all litter, practise low-impact camping and avoid setting up your tent in the spruce groves. Stay on designated trails to minimize vegetation damage.

From the parking lot on Rosander Main the trail winds down a series of steep switchbacks to the valley floor. Before the start of the switchbacks look for several large cedars. Black bears forage in areas like this, gorging themselves on berries. The animals will normally shy away from people, but they can be unpredictable and dangerous. Give them a wide berth. Hike slowly and give yourself time to savour the surroundings. From the trailhead it's between forty-five minutes to an hour to reach the creek.

On the flats at Carmanah Creek the route splits at what is known as the Camp Heaven Junction. Cut left here and watch for a side path to a huge fallen tree 70 m (230 ft) long. Many visitors set up at nearby Camp Heaven, on the gravel bars of the creek. Take note that Carmanah Creek can rise quickly in heavy rains to flood many of the gravel bars and low-lying regions.

Just up from the camping area is a second side trail to a Sitka spruce with a diameter of 3.5 m (11.5 ft). Farther along is a hollow spruce stump large enough to cram ten people in. Those hiking further upstream can seek out several groves of large trees, including one featuring the Carmanah Triplets, a trio of spruce. A right at the Camp Heaven Junction accesses the trail to Heaven Grove, a group of spruce trees that includes one 81 m (265 ft) tall. You can also wind downstream to some big western hemlock trees. Beyond here the trail is closed. The Parks Branch has imposed this restriction for public safety reasons and to protect the Carmanah Giant's fragile root network from the boots of too many hikers. Equally impressive spruce trees, such as the Carmanah Triplets, are found in less-sensitive areas and are more accessible to Carmanah Valley visitors.

Contacts

MacMillan Bloedel (Cameron/Franklin Division) (604) 723-9471; B.C. Forest Service (Port Alberni) (604) 724-9205; B.C. Parks (Malahat District) (604) 387-4363; B.C. Parks (Victoria) (604) 387-5002; B.C. Parks Public Information Officer (Victoria) (604) 387-4609; Western Canada Wilderness Committee (Victoria) (604) 388-9292.

Maps/Guides

MacMillan Bloedel TFL 44 Recreation and Logging Road Guide (East Map); Western Canada Wilderness Committee Carmanah guide; Guide to the Forestland of Southern Vancouver Island (LCCFO); Parks Branch Carmanah Pacific Provincial Park brochure; Hiking Guide to the Big Trees of Southwestern British Columbia (Stoltmann/Western Canada Wilderness Committee); National Topographical Series: 92C/10 Carmanah Creek (1:50,000); 92C/15 Little Nitinat River (1:50,000); Provincial Map: Regional Map #2 Parksville/Tofino (1:125,000).

Nearest Services

Port Alberni; Lake Cowichan area.

TRIP 11: Flora Lake Backroads

In Brief

Many backwoods browsers are familiar with Sarita Main, the backroad from Franklin Camp to Bamfield, but there is an alternate route. Starting near the top end of Nitinat Lake, Flora and Central South mainlines will take you to the Bamfield region and by several trout lakes, one with a wilderness campsite.

Access

Drive to the west end of Cowichan Lake and follow Nitinat Main 18.5 km (11.5 mi) to the Nitinat Junction. Turn right, cross the Nitinat River bridge and continue another 8.5 km (5.3 mi) on South Main to the Flora Main junction. (You can also come in from Port Alberni. The cutoff is about 13 km (8.1 mi) south of Franklin Camp.) Flora Main and Central South Main are active hauling roads with narrow stretches and blind corners. MacMillan Bloedel (Mac/Blo) suggests travelling these arteries after 5:00 p.m. on weekdays. Heavy industrial traffic may be encountered on South Main. Gravel mainlines are in good shape. Secondary roads are good-to-fair.

Description

Whenever I travel to Bamfield, I usually make a loop-run there: driving one way on Sarita Main (the main road) from MacMillan Bloedel's Franklin Camp; the other along Flora Main and Central

South Main. The latter route passes Flora, Crown and Rousseau lakes and runs through parts of three river valleys—Little Nitinat, Klanawa and South Sarita.

There are two ways to approach Flora Main. Travel to the west end of Cowichan Lake and over to the head of Nitinat Lake. At the signposted Nitinat Junction, swing right to cross the Nitinat River bridge and continue 8.5 km (5.3 mi) to the start of a paved section of South Main. Island adventurers heading in from Port Alberni will wind south about 13 km (8.1 mi) beyond Franklin Camp to the turn-off. (*Island Adventures*: Trip 10.) Swing onto Flora Main and reset your vehicle's trip meter to zero.

A wooden bridge crosses the Little Nitinat River. To the left sits an aging trestle from the days of rail-logging. Small trees have gained a foothold on the weathered timbers of the span. The Little Nitinat has created deep pools at the base of the trestle. In the heat of the summer a scramble down the rocks rewards swimmers with a chilling, yet invigorating roadside diversion. On the right-hand side of the road there is a small gravel pit. A rugged trail winds along the Little Nitinat River from here. When the river is low, you can wade up-stream quite a distance.

Just beyond the gravel pit the road splits. Fauna Main is to the right; keep left on Flora Main. The route follows a ridge on the Little Nitinat River's west side. Avoid any obvious side roads. At km 5.3 (mi 3.3) watch for the access to Flora Lake and its wilderness campsite. This site has been visited for decades by campers, anglers and back-roaders. A handful of campsites—pull-outs right on the access road—are spread out on Flora Lake's south side. To reach the lake itself, short, sometimes steep trails drop down to lakeside at several points. A rather tippy dock provides a platform for shore casters or swimmers.

Flora Lake has been regularly stocked with rainbow trout. Anglers can also try for cutthroat trout. Trout fishing is best in the spring and fall. Cartop boats can be easily launched. The Flora Lake campsite is one of the older B.C. Forest Service (BCFS) recreation sites, managed with the assistance of MacMillan Bloedel. In the off-season you may be the only one there. Should you stop here for a day or more, remember to carry out all your trash and leave your campsite clean for the next visitor. User-maintained sites benefit from everyone's continued efforts.

Flora Main skirts the north side of the lake to Upper Klanawa Main, which comes in on the left. The latter is an active mainline that runs up the East Klanawa River Valley. This backroad passes close to

Fishing is best at Flora Lake in the spring and fall.

Arthurs and Dorothy lakes before rejoining Flora Main as Branch 265. At km 12.9 (mi 8) the road splits. To the right is Central North, a hauling road that connects with Sarita Main, just east of Sarita Lake. Keep left onto Central South Main.

The road runs through logged areas and hilly terrain to Branch 139 (km 23.8/mi 14.8). This sometimes active logging road heads north along the South Sarita River to meet Sarita Main, west of Sarita Lake. There are some great views of Poett Heights and the Somerset Range along the way. Central South Main skirts Rousseau Lake to a major junction with Klanawa Main, southeast of Pachena Lake. Years ago I explored this mainline up to the then-new bridge over the west fork of the Klanawa River. At that point the road ended. Today Klanawa Main goes right to the Klanawa River to loop back onto itself as Darling Main. These logging roads are dangerously close to the West Coast Trail and are visible from the trail at several points, notably at the Klanawa River mouth.

Central South Main curves north to Sarita Main. The route passes Pachena Lake, the Between-the-Lakes bypass and a picnic site and boat launch on the northeast corner of Frederick Lake. Anglers casting from shore at these lakes have to be precise in their efforts to avoid lake-bound deadheads and fallen trees. Both lakes contain cutthroat and rainbow trout. Several primitive paths wind down to lakeside. In wet weather, gum boots will help keep your feet dry.

Around the 34-km (21-mi) mark you will hit Sarita Main. A left goes 15 km (9.3 mi) to Bamfield; a right will bring you back to Franklin Camp, about 30 km (18.6 mi) away. Should you decide to explore the Flora Lake backroads, bear in mind that MacMillan Bloedel has been active in the region. Industrial traffic (including loaded logging trucks) and loggers are often in radio contact with each other; most backroaders aren't. To avoid abrupt confrontations on these back-roads on weekdays, it is best to travel after the crews have shut down for the day. On weekends, holidays or summer shutdowns, you will only have to contend with fellow backwoods browsers.

Contacts

MacMillan Bloedel (Cameron/Franklin Division) (604) 723-9471; B.C. Forest Service (Port Alberni) (604) 724-9205.

Maps/Guides

MacMillan Bloedel TFL 44 Recreation and Logging Road Guide (East Map); Guide to the Forestland of Southern Vancouver Island (LCCFO); B.C. Forest Service Port Alberni Forest District Recreation Map; National Topographical Series: 92C/14 Barkley Sound (1:50,000); 92C/15 Little Nitinat River (1:50,000); Provincial Map: Regional Map #2 Parksville/Tofino (1:125,000).

Nearest Services

Bamfield; Port Alberni.

TRIP 12: An Off-Season Hike to Tsusiat Falls

In Brief

The majority of West Coast Trail visitors come in the warmer months, yet many hikers prefer the off-season for its greater solitude. You have to carry extra clothing and be ready for diminished daylight hours and the permeating evening chill, but for many, such a trip is worth the effort.

Access

From Port Alberni or Victoria follow the logging mainlines to Franklin Camp. Climb the hill and follow the Bamfield Road for about 41 km (25.5 mi) to the West Coast Trail entrance. (*Island Adventures*: Trips 10 and 14.) Industrial traffic may be encountered on these backroads.

Description

A few years ago a friend of mine, fresh from a stint teaching English in Japan, returned to B.C. and started talking about our heading off to the West Coast Trail. I readily agreed and it wasn't long before our pre-trip planning and preparations were done and we were en route to Bamfield. Trail ferry services would not be available, so our plan was to hike from Pachena Bay to Tsusiat Falls, base there and day-hike to other areas.

We geared up for possibly severe conditions. That meant extra clothes and our winter sleeping bags among other things. Not every traveller is adequately prepared for the often unyielding weather

*Tsusiat Falls is a highlight on
the West Coast Trail.*

conditions on Vancouver Island's west coast. Severe storms, surging in from the Pacific Ocean, can pound the shoreline—even in the summer. A growing number of hikers, caught in adverse weather, ditch gear to lighten their loads as they struggle back to civilization. Some castoffs have included food, sleeping bags, even entire packs. There are those who feel a hike along the West Coast Trail, no matter how far, is best suited for the summer months; others prefer the off-season. Hiking all or part of the West Coast Trail is extremely popular; maybe too much so. Summer overcrowding at the "tent cities" that spring up at high-use campsites (such as Tsusiat Falls or Michigan Creek) diffuses the wilderness atmosphere. Overuse in recent years has led to vegetation and trail damage, as well as an increase in litter left behind by careless campers. Sanitation problems have been alleviated somewhat by more comfort stations along the 77 km (47.8 mi) route.

Parks Canada now requires advance reservations for the free overnight permits they issue and has been forced to limit hiking starts from either the Port Renfrew or Pachena Bay trailhead to fifty-two a day (between May 1 and September 30). Reservations for each season can be made **by phone only** starting March 1 at (604) 728-1282. It certainly seems strange having to reserve a time for a wilderness hike. Pacific Rim National Park rangers will have their hands full monitoring these regulations, which also include paddlers heading to the Nitinat Triangle lakes in the daily quota. Similar calculated restrictions, in the form of staggered canoeing starts, were required in the Cariboo region's Bowron Lake Provincial Park. On our trip we would avoid all the rigamarole, since it was October.

We made good time on the first stretch to Pachena lighthouse, even though our shoulders became a little sore from our heavy packs. We dropped down to the first beach at Michigan Creek and scouted out a campsite. The sun would be down soon and we wanted to be set up when the evening chill became evident. There was no sign of rain and the long-range forecasts were promising, but out on the west coast, you can never be sure.

The trail from Michigan Creek to the Darling River follows the beach. We were facing a high tide the next morning when we set out. The boiler from the *Michigan*, a ship that went aground in 1893, was almost covered by the sea. The high water kept us up near the tree line. There were plenty of fallen trees to skirt, and in a couple of places we dodged incoming swells. Some stretches were sandy; others rocky. By the time we neared the Darling River, part of the sandstone shelf was exposed. Whenever we could, we cut out onto the shelf where the going was easier. We were forced into the cable car at the river. Sometimes you can hop across the stream on large rocks.

We discovered the trail between the Darling River and Tsocowis Creek had been recently cleared and was in fairly good shape. There were two hills—one right after the Darling River, the other near Orange Juice Creek, where the trail cut inland to avoid a headland. Smaller bog streams and creeks created countless wet and muddy spots. Some of these obstacles were skirted on old planking. We noticed bear droppings on the trail—some very fresh—and kept up a banter to alert the animal of our presence. Bears frequently amble down coastal trails foraging for food. Many hikers who frequent bear territory string a bell on their backpacks.

At Tsocowis Creek we climbed up a steep bank to the stairs. The first few steps were in bad shape. Sections were damp and very slippery. This is one of several segments of the route where impassable headlands preclude beach travel. A spectacular sandstone gorge is visible from the suspension bridge over Tsocowis Creek. A similar viewpoint is to be had at the Billy Goat Creek bridge, further south. This part of the trail runs high along a bluff. We had to watch our step on the stairs near Trestle Creek. The bridge over the creek had been washed out. Parts of it were still scattered about—on, around and under large logs. We gingerly made our way across the stream and had to use a hand rope to climb up a slick slope to the trail. Beach access required scrambling over mammoth driftwood and large wave-worn boulders—we stuck to the trail.

At several points further along you can cut down to the beach. The going is sometimes tedious, especially carrying a heavy pack on soft sand, but the seascapes are breathtaking. Klanawa River is pass-

The lure of the wilderness beaches attracts countless West Coast Trail hikers.

able at low tide. The cable car must be used at high tide. The river mouth is constantly changing. Newer logging roads and cutblocks are now visible from certain spots along the Klanawa beach. Such reminders of the frenzied cutting of Vancouver Island's old-growth forests do little to enhance the wilderness experience many people seek on hiking adventures to areas like the West Coast Trail.

The old linesman cabin at Klanawa is in poor shape, but one's perspective changes when torrential downpours and high winds buffet the coastline. One bridge, between Klanawa and Tsusiat Falls, required slow going, but soon we had reached the side trail to Tsusiat Falls, one of the West Coast Trail's scenic highlights. The steep ladders leading to the beach were treacherous. Part of one section had rotted away. We made it down in one piece and hiked over to the falls. We had the beach and falls to ourselves—one of the benefits of off-season hiking. Within the hour we had the tent up and supper on the way. It was easy to tell that the falls area had seen its usual glut of campers over the summer by the dearth of firewood. Large logs lay strewn about, but smaller pieces of driftwood were scarce. We scavenged along the high-tide line for our wood supply. The sunset that night turned Tsusiat Falls into a golden cascade. Later we were lulled to sleep by the roar of the falls and rhythmic waves breaking on the sandy beach.

From the falls area you can follow the beach below the sandstone headland. Time the tides right, though. You can beach walk all the way to Tsusiat Point and Hole-in-the-Wall, one of the better-known trail highlights. At lower tides you can work your way right through the sea-carved opening in the rocks. A mini-cave is close by. If the seas aren't co-operating, you'll be forced to climb in behind Hole-in-the-Wall to reach the next beach. The short bypass trail rises quickly to a height of land and viewpoint from which you can take in two surf-lashed beaches. In the fall the commercial fishing fleet will be out, working in the vicinity of Nitinat Bar. We rarely felt alone on our trip; seiners, trawlers, helicopters and float planes zipped back and forth, just offshore. One night it appeared as if the whole fleet was passing by; innumerable boat lights bobbed and twinkled out on the horizon.

We saw a couple of hiking parties pass by over the three days we spent on the trail, but for the most part there were few foot travellers. The weather held and there was no rain but the dampness and moisture in the early morning and evening still threatened to soak anything left out in the open. We kept our gear dry by stashing everything in plastic bags.

Our last night was spent back at Michigan Creek. On our way out to Pachena Bay the next day we stopped at the Flat Rocks lookout where hundreds of sea lions lay basking on the rocks. Before heading down the backroads to Victoria, we stopped at the pub in Bamfield to sample the pub fare—a fitting conclusion to our off-season adventure on the West Coast Trail.

Contacts

Pacific Rim National Park (Ucluelet) (604) 726-7721; MacMillan Bloedel (Cameron/Franklin Division) (604) 723-9471.

Maps/Guides

West Coast Trail Map (1:50,000) (Maps B.C.); *Pacific Rim Explorer* (Obee/Whitecap); *The West Coast Trail and Nitinat Lakes* (Sierra Club of B.C./Douglas & McIntyre); *Canadian Tide and Current Tables: Vol. 6* (Canadian Hydrographic Service); National Topographical Series: 92C/10 Carmanah (1:50,000); 92C/11 Pachena Point (1:50,000); 92C/14 Barkley Sound (1:50,000); Provincial Map: Regional Map #2 Parksville/Tofino (1:125,000).

Nearest Services

Bamfield.

TRIP 13: Horne Lake Backroads

In Brief

Nestled in the mountains west of Qualicum Beach is Horne Lake. The region is popular with anglers and backwoods browsers. Spelunkers can explore undeveloped caves at Horne Lake Caves Provincial Park. A private campsite is located near the park entrance. Spider Lake Provincial Park is a favourite day-use destination. The Big Qualicum Hatchery on Highway 19 draws countless area visitors, particularly in the fall when the salmon return to the Big Qualicum River.

Access

Horne Lake Road meets Highway 19 north of Qualicum Beach. This well-signposted gravel backroad is in good-to-fair condition. You may encounter muddy sections in wet weather.

Description

Island adventurers will enjoy travelling along the Horne Lake backroads. You can access Horne Lake, for fishing and swimming or spend a day at nearby Spider Lake Provincial Park. At the west end of Horne Lake, spelunkers explore cave networks near the Big Qualicum River. Watch for the Horne Lake Caves and Spider Lake signpost on Highway 19, just north of the Horne Lake Cafe. Cut onto Horne Lake Road and reset your vehicle's trip meter to zero. The road climbs a hill to an intersection (km 0.9/mi 0.6). A left here goes back to Highway

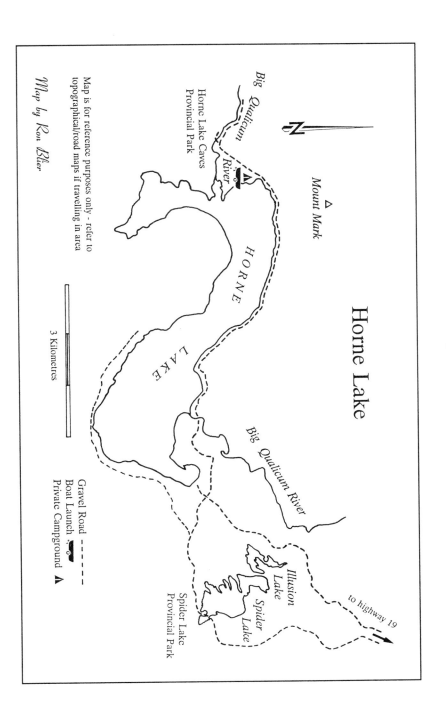

Horne Lake

Big Qualicum River

Horne Lake Caves
Provincial Park

△ Mount Mark

H O R N E

L A K E

Big Qualicum River

Illusion
Lake

Spider
Lake

Spider Lake
Provincial Park

to highway 19

Map is for reference purposes only - refer to
topographical/road maps if travelling in area

3 Kilometres

Gravel Road   - - - - -
Boat Launch
Private Campground   ▲

Map by Ron Blier

*A visitor peers into the depths
of a cave-mouth at Horne Lake
Caves Provincial Park.*

19. Keep right and cross the railway tracks. There is a short paved stretch and then, near the power lines, the gravel starts again.

The signposted left turn for Spider Lake Provincial Park is at km 3.2 (mi 2). In fact there are a couple of other side roads ahead that can also be followed to Spider Lake. Stay right on Horne Lake Road and follow the signs for the caves and private campsite at Horne Lake's west end. Years ago there were few roadside markers and on my first visit to the region I found myself baffled by the profusion of roads. Today it is much easier for travellers to find their way.

Some of the roadbed is on sandy soil. This can be a welcome change from the sometimes bumpy gravel of most Island backroads, but during heavy rains these parts of the route become slick and muddy. A second road (on the left) to Spider Lake meets Horne Lake Road at km 4.5 (mi 2.8). You'll reach a major intersection at km 7.4 (mi 4.6). Straight ahead leads to private cottage country. A left winds back to Spider Lake and accesses Horne Lake's south side. Turn right for Horne Lake Caves Provincial Park.

Take care on the approach to the one-lane bridge (km 9.3/mi 5.8) over the Big Qualicum River. Anglers will find water access nearby. Small trailered boats can be launched with care from the rough shoreline. At certain times of the year, you may run the risk of getting stuck in soft sand and gravel. The lake has been stocked with steelhead and cutthroat trout. You can fish year round, but peak times are in the late spring and fall.

Near the launch point is the dam blocking the natural outlet of Horne Lake. A sluice gate controls water flow from the lake into the Big Qualicum River. Water temperature is regulated from three water-intake levels, effectively protecting Big Qualicum River from flood and drought, and greatly increasing the survival rates of fish fry. All species of salmon return to the river, as do steelhead and sea-run cutthroat trout. A trip to the Horne Lake area is not complete without a stop at the Big Qualicum Hatchery, back near the start of our backroads jaunt, just off Highway 19.

The road continues west to pass more lakeside cottages and runs directly beneath the precipitous cliffs of Mount Mark. Scattered trees cling precariously to jagged creases in the towering rock walls. A private campsite is on the left at km 15 (mi 9.3). Many visitors camp here and daytrip to regional points of interest. The campground has a good boat launch that accommodates larger trailers.

You'll reach the Horne Lake Caves Provincial Park parking lot around the 16-km (9.9-mi) mark. From here you can hike to the mouth of Horne Lake Main and Lower caves. The footbridge over the Big Qualicum River is a treat on the way to the cave-mouths. The park was created in 1971. The Riverbend Cave has been gated to prevent vandalism. Reservations for guided tours of this nearly pristine cave can be arranged over the summer. (See Contacts.)

If you choose to visit Spider Lake Provincial Park, turn left at the signpost at the 3.2-km (2-mi) mark of Horne Lake Road. Reset your trip meter to zero. At km 2.1 (mi 1.3) you'll reach Turnbull Road. A right here heads west to Horne Lake Road. Watch for Lakeview Road (km 3.4/mi 2.1) and cut right. Just under the 4-km (2.5-mi) mark is a small parking area close to Spider Lake's southeast fringe. The main parking area is accessed along a short side road at km 4.5 (mi 2.8). The gate is locked between 11:00 p.m. and 7:00 a.m.

Spider Lake Provincial Park was created in 1981, and is for day-use only. Lakeside trails and a gently sloping, grassy shoreline make it an ideal spot for a family picnic. Summer swimming is popular at the sandy beach and the lake is known for its good bass fishing. Several restrictions apply: no smallmouth bass under 35 cm (14 in) may be kept, and only canoes, kayaks or rowboats may be used on the lake—no powerboats. Some visitors head over to the lake's northwest tip and climb over a hump of land to the Illusion Lakes.

Some friends and I were at Spider Lake when a front surged through. Somewhat surprisingly, there was little rain—but strong, gusty winds soon churned up even the smaller coves of Spider Lake.

A pair of canoeists appeared around a point and then hovered in the lee of an island. During a fleeting lull they dug in their paddles and scurried back to their launching point. The limbs of the trees near the picnic sites were whipped into turmoil and we were instantly showered with falling needles and tiny branches. Later, with the winds still blowing, we drove along Horne Lake. Spider Lake seemed calm in comparison to water conditions out on much larger Horne Lake. Steep, unpredictable, bathtub-like waves were evident in the shallower bays. Wave trains had developed in the more exposed sections and the swirling winds shifted direction constantly.

From the Spider Lake entrance you can continue west to a junction (km 5.4/mi 3.4). The right fork intersects the Horne Lake Road at the 7.4-km (4.6-mi) mark. The route to the left skirts the south side of Horne Lake to a dead end. On one backroads run, a friend and I hoped to venture down an old road and up the valley to the saddle between Mount Horne and Mount Wesley. Our hope of discovering a vista of Cameron Lake was thwarted by a locked gate. We did journey a short distance beyond Horne Lake Caves Provincial Park to a bridge over the Big Qualicum River. Here the river churns over a waterfall to a deep canyon pool. The road continues on to the confluence of Roaring and Rosewall creeks. You can work your way along to Highway 19, near Mud Bay. We saved that adventure for our next exploration of the Horne Lake backroads.

Contacts

B.C. Parks (Parksville) (604) 248-3931; B.C. Parks Public Information Officer (Victoria) 387-4609; Canadian Cave Conservancy (Victoria) (604) 757-8541; Horne Lake Caves Tours (604) 757-8677; Big Qualicum Hatchery (604) 757-8412; B.C. Forest Service (Port Alberni) (604) 724-9205.

Maps/Guides

Canadian Cave Conservancy Horne Lake Caves brochure; B.C. Forest Service Port Alberni District Recreation Map; National Topographical Series: 92F/7 Horne Lake (1:50,000); Provincial Maps: 92F/SE Port Alberni (1:125,000); Regional Map #2 Parksville/Tofino (1:125,000).

Nearest Services

Qualicum Beach area.

TRIP 14: Mount Arrowsmith Backroads

In Brief

Backwoods browsers will enjoy a journey along the backroads near Mount Arrowsmith, east of Port Alberni. Pass Main snakes up to alpine hiking within Mount Arrowsmith Regional Park, and some spectacular vistas. Cameron Main accesses the trail to Labour Day Lake, a favourite destination of local anglers.

Access

Near the Alberni Summit on Highway 4 watch for the Mount Arrowsmith Regional Park signpost and cut onto Summit Main. The route follows gravel mainlines that are usually in good shape. Pass Main is steep, with long grades and several switchbacks. The road to Labour Day Lake is in good-to-fair shape. Seasonal washouts may render the route impassable for a time.

Description

Mount Arrowsmith stands guard over the Alberni Valley, its rocky ramparts visible from miles away. MacMillan Bloedel backroads close to the mountain appeal to many Island adventurers. One route goes up to Mount Arrowsmith Regional Park. Another keeps to relatively lower ground and heads east to the Labour Day Lake trailhead near Mount Moriarty. This backroads jaunt starts near the Alberni Summit on Highway 4, east of Port Alberni. Watch for the signposted

Pass Main, up Mount Arrowsmith, leads to a spectacular vista of the Alberni Valley.

junction with Summit Main and reset your vehicle's trip meter to zero when you leave the highway.

At km 2.7 (mi 1.7) Summit Main meets Cameron Main. A right here runs 8.5 km (5.3 mi) (mostly downhill) to the Bamfield/Port Alberni Road. Bainbridge Lake is passed en route. No angling from boats is allowed and the lake has an age restriction: no one over 16 or under 65 years of age can fish its waters. A trail winds in to the lake and the shoreline casting spots. Keep left onto Cameron Main for Mount Arrowsmith Regional Park and the Labour Day Lake trail.

Just over the 6-km (3.7-mi) mark the road negotiates a switchback at Yellows Creek. It's in the next stretch that the rocky heights of Mount Arrowsmith suddenly loom above the trees. Near Cop Creek secondary roads lead up to Henry and Kammat lakes on the McLaughlin Ridge. The road approach closer to the lakes can be rough and may require a high-slung vehicle or 4 x 4. There are user-maintained wilderness campsites at both of these sub-alpine angling destinations. Henry and Kammat lakes were stocked with steelhead fry in the mid-1980s. Best fishing occurs between July and September. At km 9.9 (mi 6.1) you'll reach the Cameron River bridge and a picturesque view upstream and down. Cross the bridge over to the river's north side.

The Pass Main junction is at km 10.4 (mi 6.5). This is the turn for Mount Arrowsmith Regional Park, known for its excellent alpine hiking trails. When the snows are gone, hikers can choose from a number of challenging routes. Pass Main climbs to the park via a series of long, steep switchbacks. You can even take a shortcut, if you dare. Most travellers stick to the main road and avoid the short, but even steeper bypass halfway up the mountain. At each of three sharp corners, visitors are treated to an exceptional panorama of the Alberni Valley and the mountains beyond. On a clear day you can easily identify the head of Alberni Inlet, Sproat Lake and the south end of Great Central Lake.

I vividly recall one trip with a fellow outdoorsman that took us up Pass Main. On one of the grades it became obvious that the sharp rocks didn't particularly like my car's tires. I was able to reach a level stretch where the flat tire was removed and switched with one of two spares I was carrying. It proved to be the most scenic spot I've ever replaced a flat tire, what with the great view west.

A solitary tree stands on a clearcut slope near the third viewpoint (km 16.9/mi 10.5). From below it looks like the dead tree has been painted white. As you pass by though, you'll see that what seemed to be paint is actually the tree trunk, with its bark peeled off. Years of exposure to the elements have bleached the wood. Beyond the lone tree the mainline veers east to yet another switchback. It's not uncommon to see a number of vehicles parked at the roadside. One area trail up Mount Cokely starts nearby. Soon the road enters the regional park and runs through a patch of old-growth forest. At km 18.7 (mi 11.6) a side road to an upper alpine area swings off to the right. These days it's not uncommon to see visitors on mountain bikes on some of the older roads. The main entrance to Mount Arrowsmith Regional Park is at km 20.6 (mi 12.8).

You can stay on Pass Main to a striking viewpoint (km 21.2/mi 13.2) that looks out onto the Strait of Georgia, Hornby, Denman and Texada islands. Some anglers head further to St. Mary's Lake, which contains both rainbow and cutthroat trout. Anglers start heading there in June, right after the ice and snow melt. Cartop boat launching is possible next to the primitive campsite.

Let's return to the Pass Main/Cameron Main junction at the 10.4-km (6.5-mi) mark. Anglers and hikers planning a visit to Labour Day Lake keep straight on Cameron Main. McLaughlin Ridge and adjacent mountains and rock outcrops hem in the river valley; McInlay Peak dominates to the south. A slide that appears to be a direct result of logging is evident in this section of the route. While the roadway has been cleared of debris and smoothed out, the mountainside still bears an indelible scar.

There are many confusing forks and intersections the rest of the way to the Labour Day Lake trailhead. As long as you remember to stay on the north side of the Cameron River, there shouldn't be any problem getting there. One road, Lake Road, is signposted. Keep left onto this secondary road just over the 15-km (9.3-mi) mark. Parts of this road can be rough, particularly after heavy rains. At one point you drive through a rock slide. Keep right at km 20.8 (mi 12.9). The road splits again at km 21.3 (mi 13.2). Go left to stay on the river's north side; to the right is Branch L520.

At km 23.7 (mi 14.7) you'll reach the roadside pulloffs close to the Labour Day Lake trail. Its start is marked by ribbons on roadside branches. The trail from the logging road to the lake is only 0.5 km (0.3 mi) in length. A thin band of old growth, a B.C. Forest Service recreation reserve, surrounds the lake. A loop trail around the lake was constructed in the early 1980s. Labour Day Lake is at an elevation of about 900 m (2952 ft). While the majority of anglers day-hike in, some carry camping gear and set up at one of the wilderness campsites. I've talked to some people who have hiked to Labour Day Lake along a rugged trail beginning in the Nanaimo Lakes region to the southeast. The route, accessed from Fletcher Challenge's M Line and Rocky Run Road, passes close to Indian Lake, just south of Labour Day Lake. I hope to explore this area in the near future.

The Mount Arrowsmith backroads will lead you to great alpine hiking routes, sometimes hard-to-get-to lakes with wilderness campsites, stunning vistas and mountain scenery. And if you're like me, one visit won't be enough.

Contacts

MacMillan Bloedel (Cameron/Franklin Division) (604) 723-9471; B.C. Forest Service (Port Alberni) (604) 724-9205.

Maps/Guides

MacMillan Bloedel TFL 44 Recreation and Logging Road Guide (East Map); Guide to the Forestland of Southern Vancouver Island (LCCFO); B.C. Forest Service Port Alberni Forest District Recreation Map; National Topographical Series: 92F/1 Nanaimo Lakes (1:50,000); 92F/2 Alberni Inlet (1:50,000); 92F/7 Horne Lake (1:50,000); Provincial Map: Regional Map #2 Parksville/Tofino (1:125,000).

Nearest Services

Port Alberni.

TRIP 15: The Six Lake Loop

In Brief

This Six Lake Loop drive northwest of Port Alberni is an excellent choice for a daytrip. There are six lakes in close proximity to each other that appeal to anglers seeking cutthroat and rainbow trout. The area's many logging mainlines and secondary spurs will intrigue backroad explorers.

Access

Take Highway 4 west from Port Alberni to Great Central Road, near Sproat Lake Provincial Park. Turn right and head 7.5 km (4.7 mi) to the foot of Great Central Lake. MacMillan Bloedel's (Mac/Blo) Ash Main begins at the Stamp River bridge. The mainline is in good condition; secondary spurs good-to-fair shape; older roads may require a 4 x 4.

Description

Many Island adventurers are familiar with the backroads that connect the Port Alberni area with the Courtenay region. There is a lesser-known circle tour of small lakes to the northwest of Port Alberni that is worth consideration—particularly if you're a fisherman or a resolute backwoods browser.

The Six Lake Loop begins at the foot of Great Central Lake. A little before the start of the logging road is the Robertson Creek Hatchery. You can tour this facility, which rears coho and chinook

You can hike a short trail down to Dickson Falls, on the Ash River.

salmon. A very successful steelhead-enhancement program is in place on the Stamp/Somass river systems. The nearby dam regulates water flow in the Stamp River and creates water storage for area mills.

Cross the Stamp River bridge onto MacMillan Bloedel's Ash Main and reset your trip meter to zero. A little way along watch for the marker indicating the trail for Patterson Lake. This is a pleasant hike at any time of the year. Around the 4.5-km (2.8-mi) mark look for the signposted turn for Sumner Lake. This route is somewhat under-maintained, although it is cleared periodically of fallen trees and the like, to permit fire access. The old road is passable in a regular vehicle, but you have to take it slowly. In rainy weather a couple of sections are prone to mudholes. Make a right 1.3 km (0.8 mi) from the mainline cutoff for Sumner Lake. The secondary road continues beyond the Sumner Lake access to pass a pretty stretch of the Ash River. Next, the road skirts Moran Lake. Despite its overall size, Moran Lake sometimes is choked with marsh grasses. Beyond Moran Lake you'll soon emerge back on the Ash Main, having travelled about 7.5 km (4.7 mi).

Directly across the mainline is Branch 83, the road on which we'll complete our loop run. If you are able to resist the option to explore the Sumner/Moran artery and keep to Ash Main, it's 6.5 km (4 mi) from the Ark Resort to Branch 83. At the 11.7-km (7.3-mi) mark you can park your vehicle and hike in to Dickson Falls on the Ash River. Make sure you park well off on the shoulder of the mainline.

Just down the road are two old branch roads, signposted as 101 and 102. The latter spur has been closed for a number of years. A friend and I once journeyed down this spur and wended our way along Dickson Lake's west side. Even then there were some problems with road conditions. Streams had undercut parts of the roadway, caving in the sides and creating tenuous spots where we carefully edged our vehicle through. Other sections had been marked by ribbons on tree branches strategically placed in deep holes and washouts. We made it all the way to Ash Lake, but time and the elements have taken their toll on Branch 102: it's now impassable, except on foot. It's easy enough to see a collapsed bridge or rough sections that might damage your vehicle. Sinkholes are another matter. Sometimes the route looks passable, but the weight of a car or truck is enough to cave in the road. Veteran backwoods browsers who frequent the older backroads carry with them a shovel and at least a come-along or winch. Getting stuck out in the wilds is no fun.

Around the 13-km (8.1-mi) mark you'll cross the Ash River bridge near Dickson Lake. The entrance to a wilderness campsite is on the left, on the far side of the span. This is private property and there are no toilets, garbage cans, picnic tables or amenities of any sort. A natural boat launch slopes into the lake. Visitors can help ensure continued public access by tidying up their site when leaving, following seasonal fire restrictions and refraining from cutting trees for firewood.

Anglers frequent Dickson Lake in the spring and fall as the trout action heats up. The lake has a number of spidery arms, each offering fishermen some seclusion. Popular methods are dragging a worm along the lake bottom at dropoffs, and either trolling or casting in lake narrows and near creek-mouths. Some of the smaller streams are hard to see; these must be located by the gurgle of their waters and a subtle change in lakeside vegetation.

At km 15 (mi 9.3) you'll reach a three-road junction. The right-hand road is overgrown and rarely used. Straight ahead leads to Willemar and Comox Lake in the Courtenay region. (Island Adventures: Trip 20.) Make a left at the junction for this trip. At km 15.5 (mi 9.6) cut left again onto a secondary spur. About 1 km (0.6 mi) along is the access road for Ash Lake. At lakeside there are a couple of parking areas from which you can launch a canoe or small boat. You could set up a small tent for an overnight stay, but many backwoods browsers prefer small camper units.

The Six Lake Loop skirts Ash Lake's east side. You can stop and try some shore casting at a number of spots, but this requires a climb down a steep bank to lakeside. Keep right at a fork (km

Seasonal steelheading is popular on many Vancouver Island streams.

18.7/mi 11.6). On one trip I explored the left spur, and quickly discovered that the route petered out; but not before crossing two creeks and some washouts. When small saplings and bushes became a threat to my vehicle's undercarriage, I parked and hiked in a little further. A gap in the trees provided a nice view of Ash Lake. Motion out on the water turned out to be some canoeists fishing the lake.

By km 20 (mi 12.4) you should be able to spot McLaughlin Lake to the left through a stand of tall trees. In this section newer culverts are in place where off-season washouts had made the road quite rough. Just under the 21-km (13-mi) mark a side road (on the left) goes up a hill. This artery eventually dead-ends at a couple of wilderness picnic sites at McLaughlin Lake. There is an alternate route to McLaughlin: stay on Ash Main, drive by Turnbull Lake—a long slender lake popular with fly casters—and cut down to McLaughlin on what locals refer to as the "high road." For this jaunt we come in on the lower road.

Beyond the McLaughlin Lake turn the route skirts Lois Lake and winds down to the access road from Lowry Lake (km 25.4/mi 15.8). It's a short way to the wilderness campsites and natural boat launch. Trumpeter swans make Lowry Lake their home over the winter months. Of all the lakes described in this backroads run, Lowry Lake has the best swimming area. The shoreline gradually slopes into the water, unlike the rocky and sometimes muddy bottoms of the other lakes. At Lowry Lake you can see the mountains bordering Great Central Lake's south side. If it's early in the season, you may even be able to pick out snow pockets, slowly decaying in shady crevices on the higher ridges.

You'll reach the intersection with Branch 83 at km 26.7 (mi 16.6). Straight ahead is a water access for Great Central Lake, used by paddlers on their way to the Della Falls trailhead at the head of the lake. Launching from this point cuts down lake travel time.

Turn left onto Branch 83 for about 10 km (6.2 mi) to reach Ash Main; swing right and follow the mainline back to the Stamp River bridge. There are several high views of Great Central Lake along Branch 83 as it winds through woodlands in the shadow of Thunder Mountain.

The Six Lake Loop is not a long one, but it provides Island adventurers with a wide choice of places to explore and lakes to fish. Anglers should note that over the summer, the fish tend to have soft flesh, making them less than ideal for eating. Prime fishing times in the area are the spring and fall. Fire closures may restrict public entry on some roads during times of dry weather.

Contacts

MacMillan Bloedel (Sproat Division) (604) 724-4433; B.C. Forest Service (Port Alberni) (604) 724-9205.

Maps/Guides

MacMillan Bloedel TFL 44 Recreation and Logging Road Guide (East Map); B.C. Forest Service Port Alberni Forest District Recreation Map; National Topographical Series: 92F/6 Great Central Lake (1:50,000); 92F/7 Horne Lake (1:50,000); Provincial Maps: 92F/SW Kennedy Lake (1:125,000); 92F/SE Port Alberni (1:125,000).

Nearest Services

Port Alberni.

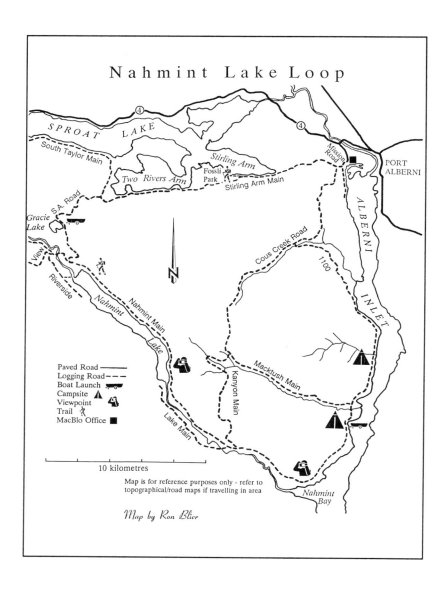

Nahmint Lake Loop

Map is for reference purposes only - refer to
topographical/road maps if travelling in area

Map by Ron Blier

TRIP 16: The Nahmint Lake Loop

In Brief

Backwoods browsers who enjoy loop tours along Vancouver Island backroads will delight in the 75 km (46.5 mi) logging road jaunt through MacMillan Bloedel forestlands west of Port Alberni. The route passes through mountainous terrain and accesses several freshwater fishing destinations and a few wilderness camping areas.

Access

Take Highway 4 west from Port Alberni to the Somass River bridge. Turn left onto Mission Road, continue past MacMillan Bloedel's Sproat Division office and up the hill to the Cous Main junction. The route follows gravel mainlines (combined-use roads). There are some steep grades. Secondary roads may be rough. Active logging areas are usually gated.

Description

A backroads adventure into unfamiliar regions arouses a keen sense of anticipation. That was the case the first time I travelled the Nahmint Lake Loop. Parts of the route I knew—the stretch along the south side of Sproat Lake and the switchback up to Gracie Lake. It was the yet-unseen sections along the Alberni Inlet and through rugged mountains near Nahmint Lake that held the intrigue.

Our starting point will be the intersection of Cous Creek Road

*Vancouver Island backroads
lead to wilderness adventure.*

and Stirling Arm Main, within a logging-road network south of Sproat Lake. Drive through Port Alberni on Highway 4. River Road parallels the Somass River to the highway bridge. Once across this span, make a left onto Mission Road. If it's a clear day, you'll be able to identify Mount Arrowsmith. This landmark stands guard over the Alberni Valley and makes great subject material for photographers; especially when its jagged heights are camouflaged with winter snows. Just beyond the entrance to the J.V. Clyne Bird Sanctuary, a wintering area for trumpeter swans, are MacMillan Bloedel's Sproat Lake Division offices. Their TFL 44 Recreation and Logging Road Guide (East Map) covers the logging roads for the Nahmint Lake Loop; you can pick up a copy at the tourist information office, right on Highway 4 as you approach Port Alberni.

About 2.7 km (1.7 mi) from the highway you'll reach a fork. The left road runs along the head of Alberni Inlet where there are more superb views of Mount Arrowsmith. Keep right and climb the short hill. The signposted turn (km 3/mi 1.9) for Cous Creek Road is at the top of the grade. (Note: Some maps and road signs indicate Cous

Main.) Cut left here and reset your trip meter to zero.

At km 7.2 (mi 4.5) there is an important cutoff. Cous Creek Road stays on the north side of Cous Creek and eventually connects with Macktush Main. Active logging is ongoing further down this artery and as one Mac/Blo employee told me: "There's not much to see on this road." Cut left onto Branch 1100 (also known as Canal Main) and cross the Cous Creek bridge.

Just over the 10-km (6.2-mi) mark is the first of many glimpses of Alberni Inlet. A clearcut on the far side contrasts starkly with the greens of the surrounding forest. At km 12.4 (mi 7.7) you'll start a long descent to sea level. Across the inlet you'll see China Creek Park, near the mouth of China Creek. Saltwater anglers often base here. At km 17.4 (mi 10.8) watch for the steep entrance (on the left) to the B.C. Forest Service (BCFS) Arden Creek campsite with seven user-maintained sites. There is no boat ramp here, but cartoppers can be carried down to the water.

The road meets Macktush Main and then curves across the Macktush Creek bridge to pass through a recent clearcut. At km 22.3 (mi 13.8) you'll reach the Bill Motyka Recreation Area, situated on private MacMillan Bloedel land. Mac/Blo recently made $300,000 in improvements to their nearby winter log dump. The logged-off areas near the site were replanted in the fall of 1989. At the peak of the summer salmon season, RV'ers and campers line the waterfront at this saltwater fishing destination. Many visitors choose to tent in a forested fringe along the water. There are comfort stations and a sometimes bustling boat launch.

Alberni Inlet has many moods. Under ideal conditions only a delicate swell disturbs its calm. At other times inlet waters can be alive with whitecaps dancing out on windswept reaches. Chop can build rapidly, especially near log booms or along sheer shoreline cliff faces. Currents can be tricky at inlet narrows or when tides battle contrary winds. Boaters with smaller craft should be wary.

The mainline, now called Nahmint Main, continues south from the recreation area through challenging terrain to Nahmint Bay, a wide coastal indentation on Alberni Inlet's west side. Here, the Nahmint River empties into the sea. Alberni Pacific Lumber Ltd. logged the lower Nahmint Valley in the late 1920s. Their railway logging extended along the river's northeast side almost up to Nahmint Lake. A stunning viewpoint (km 28.2/mi 17.5) looks out over Nahmint Bay. The first time I came upon this vista, fingers of fog were slowly groping their way inland from the coast. The sea mist hugged the contours of the mountains and valleys, giving them an ethereal look. There's a second lookout just down the road, from which you can gaze down onto the tidal flats at the head of the bay.

The region's austere topography coupled with deluging rainfalls and super-quick runoff creates instant creeks, waterfalls and flooded streams. It's easy to see why many backroads fall prey to the elements. Rock slides and washouts near Nahmint Lake have made headlines before. Most of the time the mainlines are in good shape and receive regular maintenance; problem spots are well marked. It can still be unnerving to creep by a large sinkhole that has swallowed half the roadbed. On one trip during wet weather I passed numerous waterfalls and boisterous creeks right at roadside. Each torrent sang its own clamorous song to a wild country exuding an essence of isolation.

There are countless twists and turns on the Nahmint Lake Loop. On some hills you may encounter washboard surfaces and sharp rocks. Constant traffic can build up gravel ridges in places. At many points the roads are literally cut through rock; blasting was the only way to punch in the arteries. Kanyon Main (km 33.5/mi 20.8) cuts off to the right. This mainline leads to active logging regions and hooks into Macktush Main. You'll reach Lake Main coming in on the left at km 34.2 (mi 21.2). This road crosses a wooden bridge over the Nahmint River and terminates within sight of Nahmint Lake's south end. Stately old-growth timber lines the roadway at its terminus.

Nahmint Lake, 8 km (5 mi) in length, is home to large rainbow and cutthroat trout as well as wild steelhead. Dolly Varden and kokanee are also present. The lake's adjacent woodlands are the habitat of deer, Roosevelt elk and black bear. Nahmint Main hugs the mountainsides high along Nahmint Lake's east side where several captivating viewpoints are worth some time. The lake's untouched look is blemished by logging cutblocks that have encroached almost to the lakeshore. The largest is near the lake's top end, though not all of this wide swath is a result of clearcutting; wind-throw toppled some of the trees.

At km 49.9 (mi 31) look for the Nahmint Lake Trail signpost. Locals refer to the footpath as the Anderson Trail as it is close to Anderson Creek and its picturesque 20-m (66-ft) waterfall. Anglers and hikers use this steep route through stands of towering old growth to access the lake's northeast shore. Some fishermen even lug a cartopper or canoe down the trail. Heavy rains have severely washed-out the path making it hard to negotiate.

The Cous Creek bridge, along
the Nahmint Lake Loop.

At km 51.1 (mi 31.7) you'll reach a T-junction. Riverside, View and Nahmint mainlines are to the left. A side trip down these backroads is worth consideration. Let's take a quick look. Nahmint Main runs down to a bridge over the Nahmint River. Deep green pools and a mini-canyon can be viewed from the bridge. On the west side of the span is the turnoff for Riverside and View mainlines. Nahmint Main continues along the Nahmint River to an area scheduled for future logging. View Main lives up to its name; several spurs along this backroad offer excellent high vantage points overlooking Nahmint Lake.

Riverside Main extends a short distance down the lake's west side. A tanker truck access route constructed by Mac/Blo a couple of years ago ends on the banks of the Nahmint River, near its mouth. This spur is the only road link to Nahmint Lake. Working in conjunction with the Forest Service, the logging company purposely located the access point upstream from a shallow gravel bar that will deter large boat launching. This location is currently undeveloped. The establishment of a B.C. Forest Service wilderness campsite here is a future possibility. Heavy rainfall late one year and resultant river scouring of the lower floodplain created a steep 3-m (10-ft) slope at the riverside put-in.

Turn right at the T-junction for Gracie and Sproat lakes. The road negotiates a steep hill and switchback. Halfway up the grade is an exceptional look up the Nahmint River Valley. Gracie Main angles in at km 53.3 (mi 33.1). Current hauling and road construction are taking place along this spur. From this point on keep an eye out for logging trucks and industrial traffic. Some Island adventurers may prefer to tackle the active hauling roads after hours.

The mainline (now called Stirling Arm Road) soon passes Gracie Lake, a favoured destination for spring and fall anglers. A secondary spur (km 55/mi 34.2) runs down to a natural boat launch at the lake's north end. There are rainbow trout in Gracie and its waters were stocked with steelhead fry in 1982. Prior to the road access, determined fishermen slid down a slippery slope on the lake's eastern shore. The B.C. Forest Service is considering the establishment of a five-site wilderness campsite at Gracie Lake.

From Gracie Lake the road descends a steep grade to a junction at km 59.1 (mi 36.7). On the way down you'll be treated to an expansive view of the Gracie Creek Valley and Sproat Lake's Two Rivers Arm. A left onto South Taylor Main leads to the west end of Sproat Lake. Turn right onto Stirling Arm Main and at km 74.8 (mi 46.5) you'll be back at our starting point—the junction of Cous Creek Road and Stirling Arm Main.

The Nahmint area is still considered somewhat isolated, despite the fact that Port Alberni is relatively close by. The sense of remoteness one absorbs while driving area backroads keeps many travellers coming back for more.

Contacts

MacMillan Bloedel (Sproat Division) (604) 724-4433; B.C. Forest Service (Port Alberni) (604) 724-9205.

Maps/Guides

MacMillan Bloedel TFL 44 Recreation and Logging Road Guide (East Map); B.C. Forest Service Port Alberni Forest District Recreation Map; National Topographical Series: 92F/2 Alberni Inlet (1:50,000); 92F/3 Effingham River (1:50,000); 92F/7 Horne Lake (1:50,000); Provincial Map: Regional Map #2 Parksville/Tofino (1:125,000).

Nearest Services

Port Alberni.

TRIP 17: A Long Beach Hike

In Brief

Highlights of a visit to Pacific Rim National Park are the sandy beaches, big surf and unsurpassed beauty. You can choose any number of hiking destinations, but a favourite of many begins at the Schooner Cove trailhead.

Access

Take Highway 4 from Parksville to the Tofino/Ucluelet junction. (*Island Adventures*: Trip 17.) Turn right and follow the signs to the Schooner Cove trailhead and parking lot.

Description

One of the more popular regions on Vancouver Island is Long Beach within Pacific Rim National Park. A favourite hike of many park-goers begins at the Schooner Cove parking lot. The parks trail (0.8 km/0.5 mi) winds through an old cedar and hemlock forest to the camping sites at Schooner Cove. You can also reach the cove by walking along the beach from Wickaninnish Bay.

Tree-clad islands dominate the bay near the tenting ground. The largest, Box Island, is worth exploring. At low tide you can walk over the sands to the island. The sea's unrelenting force is displayed in a surge channel on the island's south side. When tides and sea conditions are right, rock scramblers can scamper over the volcanic rock

You can beach-hike from Wickaninnish Bay to Schooner Cove and beyond.

and actually complete a circuit right around the island.

Beyond Box Island an expansive beach stretches out. Sandy dunes, carpeted with kinnikinnick, spread out to the tree line. These sands can be uncomfortably warm for barefooted beach walkers in the heat of the summer. Flotsam and jetsam are deposited along the high-tide line. Visitors may find shreds of fishing nets tangled among floats, bottles and plastic debris. It's fun to stalk the gulls on the beach. Often hundreds will congregate at the high-tide line. When you get too close to them, they'll suddenly wheel up and fly to a more secluded stretch of beach. Eagles are sometimes seen effortlessly gliding above the tree line.

A friend and I once hiked this beach the day after a November storm had battered the area. The westerly winds were still exceptionally strong, and at times we were forced to walk at quite an angle to the gusts. The salty mist carried by the wind stung our faces as we moved forward. The rugged archipelago of Schooner Cove split the Pacific swell into confused wave patterns and currents. Large breakers crashed relentlessly on the shore.

Beachcombers exploring the cove's smaller islands may discover a myriad of tiny shore crabs in the shallows. These creatures scavenge the tide zones in areas where small stones or rocks are prevalent. The crabs are interesting to observe as they dart about in their sideways manner.

Eventually, the sands give way to rocks at the west end of Schooner Cove. Many beach walkers are content to end their forays here and bring out their lunches to enjoy with the sea and sand as a

The surf-lashed beaches at Long Beach lure thousands of visitors annually.

backdrop. Rock climbers and more adventurous beach explorers can continue west to Portland Point or even beyond to the secluded Radar beaches.

The route requires some rock scrambling. At one point a large surge channel must be skirted. No problem when the seas are calm. When the wind and swells are up though, roiling white water seethes up the rocky constriction to explode in a fury of spray.

Take note that high tides can cut off the beach routes for a number of hours, so it's best to tackle the rugged shoreline west of Schooner Cove when the waters are receding. Give yourself time to get back. During high winds and heavy seas, only the foolhardy will attempt any exploration of the low-lying parts of the coastline. Even passage on the higher rocks up at the salal bush lines may be treacherous in times of heavy weather. The *Canadian Tide and Current Tables: Vol. 6* will assist hikers as they plan their departure and return times for this hike.

We huddled under a poncho at one point, to keep dry when a heavy shower passed over. Suddenly there was movement in the salal bushes and a tiny head poked up, staring at us. It turned out to be a pine marten. The animal seemed quite curious and watched us for some time before disappearing in the underbrush. We worked our way west to Portland Point, where a large hump of rock protrudes out from the shoreline. We were considering climbing over to the projection, but the tidal neck connecting it to the shore seemed awfully damp, even though no waves were breaking there. We tarried a few minutes and then a surging sea rose suddenly to inundate the low-lying rocks with a white froth. We were glad we waited.

You can camp right on the beach at Schooner Cove by hiking in with a tent. Over the summer as many as eighty tents will add their bright colours to the sea-and-forest backdrop. Other visitors choose to stay at Greenpoint Campsite, south of the Schooner Cove parking lot on Highway 4. Greenpoint has facilities for RVs and camper units. Whatever location you choose as your base, you won't want to pass up a day-hike on the beaches west of Schooner Cove.

Contacts

Pacific Rim National Park (Ucluelet) (604) 726-7721; Infocentre (Highway 4) (604) 726-4212 (Easter through mid-October).

Maps/Guides

Pacific Rim Explorer (Obee/Whitecap); *Canadian Tide and Current Tables: Vol. 6* (Canadian Hydrographic Service); National Topographical Series: 92F/4 Tofino (1:50,000); Provincial Map: Regional Map #2 Parksville/Tofino (1:125,000); Environment Canada map: Pacific Rim National Park (1:70,000).

Nearest Services

Tofino; Ucluelet.

TRIP 18: Upper Quinsam Backroads

In Brief

There are a number of lakes and wilderness campsites that can be accessed from Highway 28 west of Campbell River. This is a great area for backroad exploring and fishing. Be ready to get lost—there are many confusing side roads.

Access

Take Highway 28 west from the Campbell River Island Highway junction. Argonaut Main intersects Highway 28 at km 17.7 (mi 11). Turn left onto the mainline. There may be heavy industrial traffic encountered on the first stretch of Argonaut Main. Mainlines are in good shape. Secondary roads are good-to-fair. Some older roads may require a 4 x 4. Fire closures and active logging may restrict public access.

Description

We weren't lost; we just weren't one hundred percent sure where the backroad was leading us. We were heading to Wokas Lake, one of many trout lakes on the south side of Highway 28, west of Campbell River. Argonaut Main is the main industrial road into the area, but our maps indicated an alternate spur further west on the paved road that also accessed Wokas. We missed the turn on the highway and had to backtrack to the start of the elusive artery. The surrounding forest was in deepening shadow with the onset of evening, making it

Lakeside trails, at many Vancouver Island locales, will delight the kids.

difficult to obtain a proper bearing. There was also a plethora of unmarked side roads not shown on our maps, making it even trickier to stay on course. The road suddenly dipped into a clearing and we could make out a lake in the dimming light.

"If we can see some old trestle supports in the lake, we'll know this is Gooseneck," I remarked to my travelling companion and his ten-year-old son. Sure enough, there they were, pinpointing our immediate location. It was getting rather late for our young traveller, so we asked him whether he wanted to camp for the night at Gooseneck's wilderness campsite or continue on to Wokas Lake. Peter was silent for a minute, and then, in true backwoods browser fashion, he suggested we forge ahead to Wokas. (That old road we had negotiated down to Gooseneck Lake that year is now severely overgrown. Backwoods browsers may encounter fallen limbs, mudholes, washouts and treacherous sinkholes.)

The maze of roads persisted, but somehow we reached the bridge (now removed) over Wokas Lake's outlet stream. Problem: a heavy steel cable imbedded in massive concrete blocks barred our route. The bridge was unsafe for vehicles and had been barricaded for safety purposes. That fact didn't help us much. We had to reverse direction again and head east to Argonaut Main to finally reach the secondary spurs to Wokas Lake's wilderness campsites. Here we would base for a few days of canoe explorations and fishing.

The gateway to the Upper Quinsam backroads is Argonaut Main.

From this private industrial road you can access a variety of area lakes. Take Highway 28 (Gold River Highway) west from Campbell River. (*Island Adventures*: Trip 26.) You'll pass Echo Lake, popular with shore casters, en route to the intersection with Argonaut Main (km 17.7/mi 11). Turn left and reset your vehicle's trip meter to zero. The first stretch of the route is wide, but in wet weather it can be extremely muddy; ore trucks from the Quinsam Coal Mine haul down the industrial mainline and frequently churn things up. At a fork (km 5.8/mi 3.6) keep right. A one-way section starts just over the 7-km (4.3-mi) mark. There is a junction at km 7.7 (mi 4.8). Keep right onto Branch AR2 for the primitive campsite at Gooseneck Lake and continue just under 2 km (1.2 mi) to another spur road. Turn right again. A bumpy but passable backroad winds just over 1 km (0.6 mi) to the lake. In the off-season, you may have to dodge a number of waterholes.

I've been in to Gooseneck Lake a couple of times. On one trip a fellow outdoorsman and I came in from the south on spurs that were a little more obvious than the overgrown roads to the north. We carefully walked out on the decaying trestle timbers almost to the far side of the bay, taking the opportunity to cast out lines at several fishy-looking spots. Gooseneck has been stocked with cutthroat trout. You can fish there with good results right through the summer, though the best times are April through June, and September and October.

Let's go back to the 7.7-km (4.8-mi) mark on Argonaut Main. Middle Quinsam Lake can be reached by heading east on spur roads. Branch AR3 stretches along the north side of Middle Quinsam where there are a couple of wilderness recreation sites. B.C. Environment stocked the lake with steelhead fry in the early 1980s.

Straight ahead on Argonaut Main will take you to the side roads to Wokas Lake. When you reach a swampy area and a series of ponds, look for passable side roads on the right that connect with another spur parallelling the east side of the lake. The main access is Branch AR61. There are a number of user-maintained sites at Wokas Lake. My favourite is the one closest to Wokas Channel, the narrow water link from Wokas to Upper Quinsam Lake.

Anglers can easily work Wokas Lake, even when the wind has stirred up the much larger Upper Quinsam Lake. The latter is more susceptible to wind-induced wave action—a fact to be noted by neophyte paddlers. On calm days Upper Quinsam is a canoeist's treat, with quiet coves and several islands to visit. The mountain backdrop is spectacular; except for the disused Argonaut Mine, clearly displayed on the mountainside near Mine Creek. Denuded of trees, the

A spillway and dam on the Quinsam River, north of Wokas Lake.

slopes are now a bleak, rock-strewn incline scarring the natural beauty of the surrounding hills. But it's easy to look beyond this scar to the pristine, snowy crowns of distant peaks.

On one trip a fellow outdoorsman and I drove down Argonaut Main all the way to the crossroads beneath the abandoned mine. Straight ahead is Mine Creek Main. We cut right onto Granite Main and drove to Branch G1000 which brought us to a somewhat overgrown spur west of Hawkins Creek. It was a bumpy, rutted route that required adept straddling of the tires and slow manoeuvring on the really rough sections to reach the shores of Upper Quinsam. We finally reached an obvious campsite at the lake's east end.

There are several lakes in the region I have yet to visit. A fellow backwoods browser beat me in to Camp Lake, west of Wokas Lake. You drive on Highway 28 to the junction with Berry Creek Road on the east side of Upper Campbell Lake. My friend journeyed there in a Volkswagen van and encountered only one problem spot along the way. He was more concerned with the many confusing unmarked side roads than a few scrapes to the undercarriage. Camp Lake is a small lake anglers can easily work in a day. A rough, natural boat launch is ideal for cartoppers.

For those who enjoy afternoon runs on logging roads, this region features countless choices for backwoods browsers. Some of the old roads require a truck or 4 x 4; others can be carefully negotiated in a regular car. Many roads shown on area maps are now impassable due to blocked or removed bridges, sinkholes or wash-outs. And not all the roads are marked on every map. If you're the curious type, you'll just have to scout out the unmarked routes by trial and error. But that's just what backwoods browsing is all about.

Contacts

Fletcher Challenge (Elk River Division) (604) 287-7979; B.C. Forest Service (Campbell River) (604) 286-9300.

Maps/Guides

Campbell River Search and Rescue Society Logging and Highway Road Map; Fletcher Challenge Elk River Division Logging Road Guide; B.C. Forest Service Campbell River Forest District Recreation Map; National Topographical Series: 92F/13 Upper Campbell Lake (1:50,000); 92F/14 Oyster River (1:50,000); Provincial Map: 92F/NW Buttle Lake (1:125,000).

Nearest Services

Campbell River.

TRIP 19: The Lure of Loon Bay

In Brief

There are many B.C. Forest Service (BCFS) campsites in the Sayward Forest and several ways to get in to them. This route starts along the Gold River Highway and winds across Strathcona Dam to Campbell Lake.

Access

Take Highway 28 west to Echo Lake. Cut right onto Fletcher Challenge Elk River mainline. Mainlines are in good shape, with industrial traffic in some stretches. Secondary spurs are rougher.

Description

The Sayward Forest northwest of Campbell River is criss-crossed by logging roads and dotted with fishable lakes. In the days of rail-logging the region was a bustle of activity. Aging remnants of huge trestles still span shadowy gorges, and pilings from logging rail lines are yet visible in many spots. Scattered throughout the area are dams, spillways, water diversions and flumes, all part of the B.C. Hydro Campbell River Development. There are almost more B.C. Forest Service recreation sites to choose from than lakes, making this area a popular destination for campers.

I sometimes wind in to the Sayward Forest from the south, using access points along Highway 28. Near the Campbell River bridge, cut onto Highway 28 following the signs for Gold River. (*Island Adventures*: Trip 26.) Just down the road is Elk Falls Provincial Park. Many visitors base at this 121-site serviced campground on the banks of the Quinsam River and daytrip through parts of the Sayward Forest.

There are many twists and turns as the highway snakes around Echo Lake. I've driven by at sunset and spotted countless risers dimpling the lake's glassy surface. Such a scene is extremely enticing to shore casters. The Fletcher Challenge Elk River Division logging yard (Camp 8) is situated at Echo Lake's west end. Elk River Main crosses the highway here. Turn right onto the mainline and set your trip meter to zero. At km 5.4 (mi 3.4), a side road angles off to the right. You can take this spur around the north side of Beavertail Lake where you'll find a couple of wilderness campsites. This lake has undergone regular rainbow trout restocking in recent years. Elk River Main skirts Beavertail's south side, where there are a few more primitive camping spots.

At km 11.6 (mi 7.2) is a major intersection. To the left goes back to Highway 28. Straight ahead, the Fletcher Challenge industrial road crosses an Upper Campbell Lake narrows and then hugs the lake's west side. Travellers planning on taking this route around the lake should contact Fletcher Challenge beforehand at their Elk River Division office. While this mainline is reasonably wide, heavy hauling by the logging company could be ongoing; in such cases, it's best to wait until truck traffic has thinned a little before setting out. Fletcher Challenge employees can provide information on the safest travel times. Turn right at the junction for Strathcona Dam. The road goes along the east side of Upper Campbell Lake (there are some nice wilderness campsites nearby) and then approaches the sluiceway and dam (km 14.3/mi 8.9).

There were four of us on my last trip through the area, travelling in two vehicles. I was the only one who had previously explored these backroads, so I knew what we'd see over the next hill—still, Strathcona Dam impressed. The element of amazement that usually hits first-time viewers fell upon my fellow travellers. We parked off on the shoulder of the road and dug into our gear for our cameras. From the dam you can look south down the top end of Upper Campbell Lake. In the distance, you'll see the Fletcher Challenge logging road bridge spanning the lake narrows. A tiny island is nearby. It's really a high point of land that escaped the flooding following the dam's completion in the late 1950s. No water was flowing in the sluiceway; it's only during periods of heavy rains that lake overflow pours over this spillway.

Make sure you gear up properly for extended paddling forays.

We saw a good deal of fish sign in Upper Campbell Lake and hoped for more of the same over the next few days. Beneath the shadow of the dam's north side we spotted the B.C. Hydro generating station and heard the thrum of its generators. From here, the Campbell River flows down into Campbell Lake. The road crosses the dam and goes down a hill. At km 15.3 (mi 9.5), we kept left onto a secondary road; a right leads to the hydro facility. This old road has a lot of curves and is quite narrow in places. Next comes the Greenstone Creek bridge, a small wooden structure over a rather boisterous stream.

By km 20 (mi 12.4), we were skirting Fry Lake. Like many area lakes, it has a fair number of dead, standing trees in its waters. Fry Lake is part of the Sayward Forest Canoe Route, a 48.4-km (30-mi) loop of nine different lakes. Linked by rivers and portage trails, this challenging paddling circuit appeals to many canoeists and kayakers. At km 20.5 (mi 12.7) we turned right to cross the bridge near Fry Lake's northwest fringe. We were temporarily delayed: a group of paddlers, no doubt fresh from the canoe route, were lashing the last canoe onto their trailer.

On the far side of the bridge we swung right to follow along Fry Lake's north side. We passed Orchard Meadows, one of the Forest Service recreation sites, and at km 24.5 (mi 15.2), we reached our planned destination: Loon Bay, a BCFS wilderness campsite on Campbell Lake. There are eight sites here, a natural boat ramp, a few picnic tables and a comfort station. A rather tippy dock was adjacent to the boat ramp. The Hydro development in this region diverts the waters of two rivers—the Salmon and the Quinsam—into Campbell Lake. The Ladore Dam at the lake's east end was completed in 1949 and raised the lake level substantially. Periodic fluctuations in water levels occur without warning at Campbell Lake; a fact we noticed one morning. The dock had been washed-out into the lake and was floating just beyond reach. It was tenuously tethered to a slim rope anchored to a post driven into the lakebed. Later, as the shifting winds swung the dock back towards shore, we secured the wooden structure once again to land.

The camping season was not quite in full swing, so we weren't surprised to find the site vacant. Over the summer though, finding room at many of the Sayward Forest BCFS recreation sites can be difficult; especially if word has spread that the fishing action there has warmed up. Plan on arriving early in the day to set up camp. We hastily set up our base of operations under scudding clouds. For me, all that involved was parking my truck on level ground and unlocking the door to the camperette. Then it was over to assist the others in the unloading of the cartop boat and popping up a tent trailer. We grabbed a quick bite to eat before gathering our fishing paraphernalia and preparing the cartopper for upcoming angling endeavours.

Blustery conditions prevented our going out that first night. Instead, we plotted our strategies for the next day beside a warming campfire that hissed in anger each time a passing shower threatened its existence. Wood was in scarce supply in the immediate vicinity, but we found ample fallen branches along one of the overgrown railbeds that ran through the campsite. It helped that we were able to load up the back of one of our pickups and transport the firewood over to our camp.

Over the next few days we indulged in many outdoor pursuits. Between the wind and heavy showers we fished, explored parts of Campbell Lake and negotiated the narrow channel into Fry Lake. When we weren't on the water, we set off on daytrips along area backroads. In a pocket cove just up from the campsite, we came upon a high trestle, camouflaged by overgrowing trees. The huge timbers still straddled a sheer ravine over which, decades ago, timber had been brought out of the woodlands via a logging railway. I took the boat out one afternoon to scout out possible fishing spots in the bay adjacent to camp. I couldn't use the outboard; there were too many stumps lurking just below the waterline. Instead, I rowed around the area for an hour or so. My casting efforts were unsuccessful, although I tried a number of fishy-looking lies. All was not in

Some anglers use a float tube on Vancouver Island lakes.

vain: by the time I brought the boat back in, I was able to keep her going on a relatively straight course—I'm not an expert with the oars.

We were camped along part of the Sayward Forest Canoe Route and took advantage of that fact and followed the constricted waterway connecting Campbell Lake with Fry Lake. We didn't see any active paddlers go by our campsite while we were based there, but out on the southwest corner of Campbell Lake, where the Campbell River pours in, a few larger powerboats worked potential strike zones. Anglers will encounter many submerged stumps and roots in the shallower sections of Campbell Lake. Boaters should keep an eye out for these hazards. The water approaches to the many BCFS campsites along the lake were "grubbed" (underwater trunks and stumps were cut short or removed entirely) by B.C. Hydro years ago, and pose no real problems for boaters.

We planned to head out via the backroads around the north shore of Campbell Lake to Loveland Bay. We'd then skirt John Hart Lake and cross the dam at the lake's east end to reach Highway 28 where it cuts through Elk Falls Provincial Park. On our final night in camp the rain let up and the wind died to a whisper. And Loon Bay lived up to its name—as dusk stole over the forest, two loons glided down into the lake waters and lulled us to sleep with their captivating calls.

Contacts

Fletcher Challenge (Elk River Division) (604) 287-7979; MacMillan Bloedel (Menzies Division) (604) 287-5000; B.C. Forest Service (Campbell River) (604) 286-9300.

Maps/Guides

Fletcher Challenge Elk River Division Logging Road Guide; MacMillan Bloedel Campbell River/Sayward Recreation and Logging Road Guide; Campbell River Search and Rescue Society Logging and Highway Road Map; B.C. Forest Service Campbell River Forest District Recreation Map; National Topographical Series: 92K/3 Quadra Island (1:50,000); 92K/4 Brewster Lake (1:50,000); 92F/13 Upper Campbell Lake (1:50,000); 92F/14 Oyster River (1:50,000); Provincial Map: 92F/NW Buttle Lake (1:125,000).

Nearest Services

Campbell River area.

TRIP 20: The Amor Lake/Gray Lake Run

In Brief

There are several ways to reach the Sayward Forest, northwest of Campbell River. One route starts on Highway 19 near Roberts Lake and accesses several B.C. Forest Service (BCFS) campsites, all on trout lakes.

Access

From Campbell River, drive 30 km (18.6 mi) north on Highway 19 to Roberts Lake. Cut left on the Forest Service road just south of the Link and Pin Museum. The secondary gravel roads are hilly and narrow with some rough sections. A truck is recommended on these arteries. Gravel mainlines are in good shape.

Description

One of the more popular destinations for Island adventurers is the Sayward Forest, northwest of Campbell River. The forests here are second growth. Extensive rail-logging decades ago removed many of the older stands of trees. The devastating Campbell River Fire of 1938 ravaged the region, destroying 30,375 ha (75,000 ac) of prime timber. The next year B.C.'s first reforestation program was initiated to help rectify the damage. There are several routes that access the Sayward Forest and travellers will find countless lakes to visit, many with wilderness campsites. For this trip we'll come in from Highway

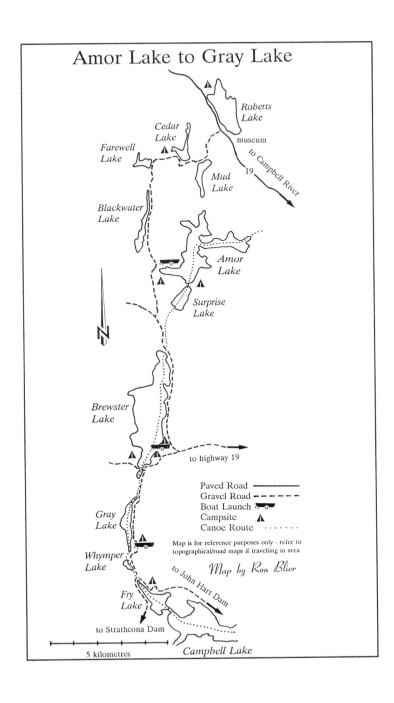

Amor Lake to Gray Lake

Roberts Lake

Cedar Lake

museum

Farewell Lake

to Campbell River

19

Mud Lake

Blackwater Lake

Amor Lake

Surprise Lake

Brewster Lake

to highway 19

Paved Road ————
Gravel Road – – – –
Boat Launch
Campsite
Canoe Route · · · · · ·

Map is for reference purposes only - refer to topographical/road maps if travelling in area

Gray Lake

Map by Ron Blier

Whymper Lake

to John Hart Dam

Fry Lake

to Strathcona Dam

5 kilometres

Campbell Lake

Jotting down trip notes is standard practise for backwoods browsers.

19 near Roberts Lake, wind down to MacMillan Bloedel's (Mac/Blo) Menzies Main and continue south to Gray Lake.

Drive through Campbell River to the junction with Highway 28 (Gold River Highway) and keep right on Highway 19 and cross over the bridge. You'll pass the Seymour Narrows lookout, Menzies Main and the Ripple Rock trailhead on the way to our backroad starting point. (*Island Adventures*: Trip 27.) About 30 km (18.6 mi) from Campbell River, watch for a gravel road on the left. It's just south of the Link and Pin Museum near Roberts Lake. Cut onto the gravel road and reset your vehicle's trip meter to zero. The first part of this run is hilly and winds by a small pond before veering west near the top end of Mud Lake. The provincial government's Corrections Branch operates Lakeview Forest Camp on the lake's west side. Many backroads near Campbell River were once railbeds, and this artery is no exception. Just over the 3-km (1.9-mi) mark you'll reach Cedar Lake and its tiny wilderness campsite. The B.C. Forest Service recently improved the lake access here. The supports of a logging trestle are visible in a narrow lake neck.

As you leave Cedar Lake, keep an eye out to the left for Muskeg Lake. You'll be able to make it out through the trees. At km 4.5 (mi 2.8) you'll hit a T-junction, close to Farewell Lake. Cut left onto Blackwater Lake Road and head south. By km 6 (mi 3.7) Blackwater Lake should be on your right. Its northern tip is so slender that you might mistake it for a small backwater or stream. Blackwater Lake soon widens out and becomes more recognizable. Determined anglers can reach Farewell or Blackwater lakes along several paths leading to shoreline casting spots.

Amor Lake is at km 9.6 (mi 5.9). There is a natural boat launch and a couple of pull-ins on the north side of Amor's outlet stream, but these are primarily overflow locales. The better camping spots are on the south side of the new bridge. Watch for the entrance at km 9.7 (mi 6). The BCFS wilderness campground at Amor Lake can be crowded on weekends; on weekdays you may find it deserted. You might be inclined to camp at the Mr. Canoehead campsite at the south end of Amor. This site, accessible by boat only, is on the Sayward Forest Canoe Route. The Amor Lake to Gray Lake backroads run passes several lakes along this popular paddling circuit: Amor, Brewster, Gray and Whymper lakes.

In addition to cutthroat trout, Amor Lake contains Dolly Varden (char) and kokanee salmon. Average size of the cutthroat is 35 cm (14 in) but sometimes you'll hook into a slightly larger fish. A small cartop boat or canoe is essential at Amor Lake so that you can access the many arms of the lake. From the campsite you have to work your way up a log-choked channel to the wider sections of the lake. Fishing can be good in many of the tiny bays on Amor Lake, but the bite is often sporadic. Early morning and sundown are good times to be out on the water.

Friends and I base at Amor Lake every few years for spring and fall cutthroat trout fishing. We have good memories from our angling stops here—except for Mike. His recollection of an Amor Lake fishing foray differs somewhat from mine and that of another angling buddy, Bill. On that trip all three of us gingerly climbed into my canoe and paddled out into the main part of the lake. We swung right to shallow water and climbed out of the canoe to first try some fly casting close to shore. Mike had been previously coached in the fine art of fly-fishing by Bill, so he was doing fairly well with his first casts. None of us had any strikes, so after an hour or so, we clambered back into the canoe and scooted off to try and find a hot spot.

Use of fly rods was impractical, so we switched to bait and bobber. In a small craft, even with only two occupants, casting must be staggered. This prevents smashing of rod tips and avoids line snags. It helps if you let your partner know when your hook is going to be airborne—so he can duck. With three in the canoe, we had to be extra careful. As sunset neared, we were casting in a cove at which we had observed a number of hatches. Suddenly the telltale rings of risers and the occasional jumper signalled the evening bite had started.

Bill and I were hooking fish almost simultaneously, but Mike was having some rough luck; not even a nibble, let alone a strike. He switched to lures, then back to bait and bobber, to no avail. His frustration level grew each time we reeled a feisty cutthroat to the canoe. (Mike got even the next day, catching that evening's largest fish.) Most anglers have suffered through similar situations. It's a part of fishing, and makes for jovial

Amor Lake is one of several making up the Sayward Forest Canoe Route.

conversation at friendly get-togethers over the winter months.

We released more fish than we kept, retaining only two or three for a tasty meal. The rest were carefully returned to their lake home. We used to put everything we caught on our stringers, but now we're more selective. To some anglers the idea of voluntary catch-and-release fishing is out of the question. They want their legal limit and keep everything they hook. Quite often they'll be the ones to miss out on a good-sized fish simply because when the larger fish were biting, they weren't fishing, having already limited out.

Blackwater Lake Road continues south from the Amor Lake campsite to hook up with Mac/Blo's Long Lake Main at km 12.2 (mi 7.6). There's a steep hill in this stretch that used to require a 4 x 4. Improvements have since been made and it's a little easier now. If your vehicle is low-slung though, you could bottom out in some of the rougher sections.

Turn left onto Long Lake Main. Just under the 13-km (8.1-mi) mark, a side road is visible on the left. This overgrown spur is a portage route up to Surprise Lake, part of the Sayward Forest Canoe Route. At km 13.7 (mi 8.5) the road crosses a small creek. You may have to creep ahead at this point as it washes out seasonally. A viewpoint at Brewster Lake is next at km 14 (mi 8.7). The distant snowcapped mountains to the west are near the White River, within Mac/Blo's Kelsey Bay Division. (See Trip 21.) Long Lake Road is full of potholes so it's slow going. During wet weather waterholes are many. The route skirts Brewster Lake's eastern fringe. Brewster Lake is one of the larger lakes in the Sayward Forest (413 ha/1020 ac) and has been regularly stocked with rainbow and cutthroat trout. Dolly Varden are also present. The fishing is good right through the summer but the best times are the spring and fall. The winds can come up on the lake so boaters should be wary.

The junction with Menzies Main is at km 18.4 (mi 11.4). You can turn left and take Menzies Main east to Highway 19. We'll swing right and continue our run to Gray Lake. There are two B.C. Forest Service campsites close to the south end of Brewster Lake. The first, Brewster Lake (km 19.5/mi 12.1), features nine campsites and a sandy beach. Remember to keep your vehicle off the beach. The Apple Point campsite (km 19.9/mi 12.4) is slightly smaller, with six campsites and a natural boat launch. This is a fairly open location and it can be windy here.

A little over the 20-km (12.4-mi) mark is the bridge at the south end of Brewster Lake. Cut left just before the span and head south. The road winds by Gray Lake's marshy north end and eventually down to the BCFS campsite, about 3 km (1.9 mi) from the Brewster Lake bridge. There are five sites here, a natural boat launch and a rickety dock. Gray Lake has recently been stocked with cutthroat trout. The lake is a treat to canoe. You can paddle down to the old logging trestle or explore the lake's slender top end.

The logging road runs another 2 km (1.2 mi) beyond Gray Lake to skirt Whymper Lake and meets Campbell Lake Road close to Fry Lake. From here you can take Campbell Lake Road back to Highway 28 at Elk Falls Provincial Park or wind along the Greenstone Forestry Road to cross Strathcona Dam and reach Highway 28 near the top end of Upper Campbell Lake. (See Trip 19.)

Contacts

MacMillan Bloedel (Menzies Bay Division) (604) 287-5000; B.C. Forest Service (Campbell River) (604) 286-9300.

Maps/Guides

MacMillan Bloedel Campbell River/Sayward Recreation and Logging Road Guide; Campbell River Search and Rescue Society Logging and Highway Road Map; B.C. Forest Service Campbell River Forest District Recreation Map; B.C. Forest Service Sayward Forest Canoe Route pamphlet; National Topographical Series: 92K/4 Brewster Lake (1:50,000).

Nearest Services

Campbell River.

TRIP 21: The Adam River/White River Loop

In Brief

Spectacular mountain scenery highlights this journey through the woodlands south of Sayward. The route provides access to the Nisnak Meadows Trail in Schoen Lake Provincial Park and connects with the backroad to Stewart Lake, popular with trout fishermen.

Access

Follow Highway 19 west of Sayward to Keta Lake. Cut left onto Upper Adam River Road (km 9.6/mi 6). The gravel mainlines are in good shape, with some hills. Heavy industrial traffic may be encountered in some sections. MacMillan Bloedel (Mac/Blo) recommends travelling after 5:30 p.m. on weekdays.

Description

Jagged mountains dominate the views along the Adam River/White River loop within MacMillan Bloedel's Kelsey Bay Division. The starting point for this run is close to Sayward. At the Sayward Junction, stay on Highway 19 to the Keta Lake rest area. A little beyond here (km 9.6/mi 6) the Upper Adam Road crosses the highway. Turn left at this point and reset your vehicle's trip meter to zero.

The Tlowils Lake turn is at km 5.7 (3.5 mi). You once could loop back to Sayward along Branch A, but now the Elk Creek bridge is out. You can still reach Tlowils Lake and its small wilderness campsite. There is a natural boat launch and good spring and fall fishing for rainbow and cutthroat trout. No gasoline motors are permitted on the lake.

As you climb up the valley, you'll catch glimpses of the snow-capped mountains and imposing rock faces which hem in the valley. Numerous waterfalls tumble down through old-growth forests to the Adam River. One of them, Phyllis Falls, is even signposted (km 10.5/mi 6.5). MacMillan Bloedel does haul along the road, so most weekday Island adventurers travel after 5:30 p.m. to avoid the industrial traffic. Most recreationists choose the weekends or holidays for their backwoods browsing.

Compton Creek Main swings off to the right at km 15.6 (mi 9.7). There are several spots in the next stretch with superb mountain views as the jagged peaks of Mount Schoen dominate the vista. It was in this area, one early May, that a backroads buddy and I were engaged in some photo taking when he motioned me over to where he was shooting. I glanced across the valley in the direction he indicated, but couldn't see anything. After much pinpointing by Bill, I finally was able to discern the cause for excitement. Standing in a slide area, looking just like a bleached stump, was an elk, with its telltale rump pointed in our direction. Bill used to hunt, and it was his keen hunter's eye that first noticed the animal's slight movement on the far ridge. For the next half hour or so we watched a family of elk slowly forage their way up the Adam River Valley. I was glad to have the binoculars along.

The road enters old growth near the eastern boundary of Schoen Lake Provincial Park. A small clearing on the left at km 21.4 (mi 13.3) serves as a parking area for the Nisnak Meadows trailhead, a hike that leads through the park's alpine meadows down to Schoen Lake. Several years ago some friends and I hiked along the Nisnak Meadows Trail. (*Island Adventures*: Trip 29.) On that trip we had purposely continued up the mainline for a closer look at the towering mountains we were seeing through the trees. A fellow traveller stopped to ask what mainline he was on and casually remarked that he was heading in to Stewart Lake for some trout fishing. We wished him luck and then went back to the Nisnak trailhead. It was a few years later that an angling buddy and I journeyed to Stewart Lake on a fishing excursion of our own.

The great mountain vistas we came upon on that first trip can be seen at km 24.4 (mi 15.2). If you decide to stop for an extended look, make sure you park well off to the right of the mainline. UA Main

A fly-fisherman tests the waters of Stewart Lake.

swings off to the right at km 25.5 (mi 15.8). You'll soon see Gerald Lake. By km 26 (mi 16.1) a massive rock slide becomes visible up ahead. From the jagged top of the mountain the slide has scoured its way down to the valley bottom in a dramatic display of Nature's force. The mainline passes close to the base of the slide, near the start of MC Main. This mainline, now called Moakwa Main, follows the north side of Moakwa Creek right below the heights of Kokummi Mountain. The road crosses the Moakwa Creek bridge and zigs and zags its way to the junction with White River Main (km 34.5/mi 21.4). To complete our loop tour, we'll cut left here and follow the White River Valley back to Sayward. But first let's take a look at the side trip to Stewart Lake.

Turn right onto White River Main. Just a little way along is the junction with Stewart Main. One of the markers at this intersection warns visitors not to feed the truck drivers! A riverside picnic site here was established by MacMillan Bloedel. This is a good place to stop for a break and take in the views of Warden Peak, Queen Peak and Victoria Peak. The latter is the third-highest mountain on Vancouver Island (2163 m/7095 ft). You'll notice the logging roads in the vicinity are built on the White River floodplain. Cut left onto Stewart Main and cross the White River bridge. We were surprised once by a pair of ducks wheeling upriver; the birds zipped by us and proceeded right under the bridge supports.

The road to Stewart Lake soon crosses a bridge over Consort Creek and climbs the creek's east side. Warden, Victoria and Queen peaks overwhelm the scenery. The further up the valley you go, the fewer the logging cutblocks become; majestic old-growth forests line the roadway. Just over 6 km (3.7 mi) from the start of Stewart Main, John Fraser Main angles off on the left. You can negotiate the abrupt hill to a high vantage point that looks out over Stewart Lake. We explored this road hoping to travel as far as John Fraser Lake to scout out possible lake access. We scrapped that idea when we encountered a severe washout. We spun around and went back to Stewart Main and continued another km (0.6 mi) or so to Stewart Lake.

A tiny wilderness campsite is located on Stewart Lake's northeast shore. A rocky boat launch slopes down into the water. On a recent visit we were travelling in an angling buddy's fully equipped camper—my first taste of camper comfort. We had to work at levelling the unit on the sloping lakeside campsite. Then we set about loading our fishing gear into the small cartop boat we had with us. No gasoline motors are allowed on Stewart Lake, and as we didn't have an electric one for the cartopper, out came the oars. Guess who was volunteered for the first shift of rowing duty?

We spent our first day on Stewart rowing around looking for a fishing hot spot. The waters right out from camp weren't producing so we slowly trolled and cast our way down to the south end. We worked the Consort Creek mouth for a few hours, casting a variety of flies. We switched to bait and bobber and tried a number of lures, all to no avail. There were no strikes and no fish sign all the way back to camp. Our luck changed the next day, with both of us catching and releasing a number of feisty cutthroat.

Let's return now to the Moakwa Main/White River Main junction at km 34.5 (mi 21.4). Nearby are several spots along the White River ideal for seasonal fish viewing. At km 38.2 (mi 23.7) you'll cross the Nora Creek bridge. On a south slope in the Nora Creek Valley a stand of old growth has been preserved by Mac/Blo to provide deer with a winter feeding area and protection from deep snows. Close by another section of forest has been spaced for spring forage for elk and deer. By km 39 (mi 24.2) you'll be driving through a pocket old-growth region set aside for elk wintering.

There are couple of steep grades in the next stretch and logging clearcuts are plentiful on the surrounding mountainsides. The White

River becomes a focal point with its rocky canyons and river pools—and a boisterous waterfall in its lower reaches. Just over the 45-km (27.9-mi) mark the road drops down a hill to reach Victoria Main. This mainline crosses the White River on a lofty bridge and then cuts right to follow the White River's south bank; a left onto the secondary spur on the far side of the bridge leads to F Branch and Salmon River Main. There is a viewpoint at the west end of Victoria Main. You can see it from White River Main as you near Nora Creek; look for an obvious notch in the tree line, high on a ridge on the river's south side.

At km 59.6 (mi 37) Branch A enters on the left. While you can't get in to Tlowils Lake via this artery anymore, you can negotiate backroads extending from Branch A to Santa Maria Lake by taking this turn. Santa Maria Lake, surrounded by second-growth forest, is an excellent destination at which to view loons. Just under the 61-km (37.9-mi) mark you'll hit Salmon River Main. A left runs north to cross Highway 19. Turn right and cut through a logging yard and follow the signs to the White River Court, just south of the Sayward Junction. You can get gas and stop for a coffee or a meal. Their store/cafe stocks the logging company recreation maps and other area travel brochures and literature.

Contacts

MacMillan Bloedel (Kelsey Bay Division) (604) 282-3331; B.C. Forest Service (Campbell River) (604) 286-9300; B.C. Parks (Parksville) (604) 248-3931; B.C. Parks Public Information Officer (Victoria) (604) 387-4609.

Maps/Guides

MacMillan Bloedel Campbell River/Sayward Recreation and Logging Road Guide; B.C. Forest Service Campbell River Forest District Recreation Map; Hiking Trails III (Outdoor Club of Victoria Trails Information Society); National Topographical Series: 92K/4 Brewster Lake (1:50,000); 92K/5 Sayward (1:50,000); 92L/1 Schoen Lake (1:50,000); 92L/8 Adam River (1:50,000).

Nearest Services

Sayward.

TRIP 22: Canoeing to a Glacier

In Brief

Experienced big-lake canoeists seeking a wilderness setting unmarked by logging will enjoy a paddle down the south end of Woss Lake. Landing spots are few, and treacherous, wind-induced wave conditions prevail. Rugged Mountain, part of the Haithe Range, towers above Woss Lake's southern fringe. Capped by glacial ice, jagged peaks and thrusting rocky ramparts dominate the mountain backdrop.

Access

This trip begins at the Woss turnoff on Highway 19 and follows gravel mainlines along Woss Lake's east side. Roads are in good-to-fair shape.

Description

Sometimes as I plan a paddling adventure, I pull out the maps and find myself looking for an unroaded wilderness, accessible only by water. These days, with the rush to extend logging roads further into Vancouver Island woodlands, regions without clearcuts and logging roads are more elusive, but not impossible to find. On northern Vancouver Island, the south end of Woss Lake still retains its wild aura. Logging roads do extend along both sides of the lake; but only halfway down. Their progress is dramatically halted by sheer topography. The logging industry is keeping its options open, however, and may punch roads through at some time in the future. Industrial encroachment could

Woss Lake paddlers should always keep an eye on the weather.

jeopardize a proposed ecological reserve at Woss Lake's south end.

Beyond the last logging cutblock, imposing mountains and precipitous rock walls tower above Woss Lake. The lake's 9 km (5.6 mi) of wilderness shoreline offers limited landing spots, and even fewer rough campsites. But with proper preparation, good timing and a healthy respect for wind and waves, experienced big-lake paddlers can journey to the head of the lake, directly beneath the rock face and glacier that caps Rugged Mountain, 1875 m (6151 ft) high.

Take the Woss turnoff on Highway 19 and reset your vehicle's trip meter to zero. Follow the road through to Woss, the tiny Canadian Forest Products (Canfor) logging community. You can stop at the Canfor office and pick up a copy of their Nimpkish Valley logging road guide. Over the summer you can make reservations for forestry tours that include a ride on an old steam locomotive. Cross the Nimpkish River bridge (km 1.4/mi 0.9) and glance to the left to see a picturesque falls on the river. Continue across the span to a signposted junction. Bear right and follow the signs for Canfor's Woss Lake campsite. At km 4.1 (mi 2.5) a right will take you over the Woss River onto the industrial road that snakes along the south side of Nimpkish River to the Zeballos Road. (See Trip 25.) The Woss Lake campsite, nestled in a grove of stately trees at the tip of the lake, is at km 4.5 (mi 2.8). This relatively large (twenty-four-site) campground is close to the Woss River, the outlet stream which empties the lake into the Nimpkish River. Trails through the surrounding forest extend from the campsite. Picnic tables and fire pits complement the sites. A big feature of this locale is the lake's sandy beach, ideal for summer wading or swimming. I've camped here a couple of times; once in early January. It is over the warmer months though, that the campsite fills up.

The developed launch ramp helps fishermen with trailered boats and cartoppers access the lake. There's also a dock. Woss Lake anglers seek cutthroat and rainbow trout as well as Dolly Varden (char). The lake has been stocked with cutthroat fry. Determined fishermen will find fish right through the summer, but best results are in the spring and fall. (Note the rainbow trout release restriction for Woss River.)

The road swings east to pass the tip of a small lake. Cut right at km 5.5 (mi 3.4) and avoid any left-hand spurs. At km 6.7 (mi 4.2) you'll skirt a bay on Woss Lake. The mainline continues along the east side of the lake to a rough dead end in a cutblock. On the way down you'll be able to see a large slide on the opposite shore. Around the 11-km (6.8-mi) mark there are a couple of lake-access points. Space is tight here, but you can set up a wilderness camp. Remember to carry out your trash and follow seasonal fire restrictions.

The day we drove up heavy showers and strong winds were stirring up the small lakes we passed along Highway 19. If they were wavy, Woss Lake would be worse. Things can get very turbulent on Woss Lake, but that's typical of any large lake on northern Vancouver Island. Visitors must pick their paddling times carefully and gear up for adverse conditions.

We inched our vehicle down a short spur and walked down to the shore of Woss Lake. There would be no canoeing that night. Large swells rolled into the bay, and out in the wider stretches whitecaps danced on the water. The clouds were breaking though, and the scattered showers were less frequent.

We did manage some paddling the next day when things were a little calmer. We kept just offshore, working our way slowly into the wind. When you're dealing with wave trains on large lakes, it's hard to resist the temptation to go with the waves when you set out; travelling with them is fast and easy. Should conditions worsen an hour or so later, you could be faced with a much longer, tiresome, and sometimes dangerous paddle back into wind and waves.

Big-lake paddlers often must deal with blustery conditions.

Fallen trees plunge down into the lake along both its shorelines. While these toppled forest giants provide some protection in blustery conditions, paddlers are often forced out into wilder waters in order to bypass obstructing branches and swaying limbs. At one point we ducked behind a massive deadfall for a short break. From here we were treated to a view toward Woss Lake's south end. We could see the massive rock face of Rugged Mountain, its higher reaches still obscured by thick clouds. We worked our way north by a few more bays, and then swung around to ride the swells back to camp.

The next day we were greeted by sunshine—and a calm lake. Our eyes were drawn again to Rugged Mountain, and this time its glacier cap was cloud-free. With binoculars out we peered at the icy sentinel, and soon were loading the canoe for a journey to lakehead. We skimmed over the glassy calm and soon had left behind the logging cutblocks on the lake's east side. Perpendicular cliffs plummeted into the lake. Snows still lingered on the top of Woss Mountain. We journeyed along the west side of Woss Lake, marvelling at the rugged terrain and pristine old-growth forest. The glacier was in view most of the way, until even it became hidden as we approached the looming cliffs immediately below it. Far above, a plunging waterfall fed by snowmelt dropped over a precipice. Avalanche scars were evident higher up on the mountain slopes.

As we had suspected from looking at area topographical maps, there were limited landing spots all the way to lakehead. There, the lake curved to the west and shallowed somewhat. At least eight streams enter the lake here. An old Indian trail followed one of them up over the divide and on to the Tahsis River. An extensive gravel bar has been formed on the east shore of Woss Lake. It was here, directly beneath the rock wall, that we landed for lunch and some fly casting against a riveting backdrop. At first glance, this setting looks like an excellent fishing spot. The best angling results though, are back at the campsite-end of Woss Lake. Over the course of the three days we spent at the lake, we saw only one other boat, working the far shoreline. The anglers trolled along the cliffs where the lake narrows but they didn't go further, and soon were scooting back to Woss's north end.

We were at the head of Woss Lake for a only short time when its mirrored surface was blurred by tiny wavelets stirred up by gusts of wind. The breeze came from the same direction as it had the previous two days. That meant we'd be heading back against both wind and waves. We decided to follow the lake's east side, while scouting possible campsites. We discovered only three practical spots for an overnight camp, the best being a jut of rock and forest next to a chattering creek.

The wind picked up, but not uncomfortably so. We made slow but sure progress, staying in less-agitated waters behind points of land. Each time we scooted into an adjoining bay, we wondered what conditions were like around the next corner. When we reached the logged-off shore, we thought the worst of the waves were behind us. However, emerging from the narrower stretches of the lake, where the shoreline curved and the lake bottom shallowed, we faced confused, bathtub-like chop and larger wave trains. We could have run for shore, accessed the logging road and walked back to camp, but we weren't shipping any water, so we stayed on the lake. This required staggered paddling and a fair bit of stabilizing, but we edged ahead to finally scrape bottom in front of our camp.

For wilderness seekers, the south end of Woss Lake is an excellent destination. Visitors should be adequately prepared while out on the water, even if they plan only a short paddling foray; wind and water conditions can change quickly. Keep in mind that on some days Woss Lake won't let you in—or out.

Contacts

Canadian Forest Products (Woss) (604) 281-2300; B.C. Forest Service (Port McNeill) (604) 956-5000.

Maps/Guides

Canadian Forest Products Nimpkish Valley Logging Road Guide; B.C. Forest Service Port McNeill Forest District Recreation Map; National Topographical Series: 92L/2 Woss Lake (1:50,000); Provincial Map: 92L Alert Bay (1:250,000).

Nearest Services

Woss.

TRIP 23: The Bonanza Lake Run

In Brief

Many backwoods browsers head to Telegraph Cove via the paved Highway 19 and Beaver Cove road. You can also take logging roads from the Woss area north to the tiny community. This 44.5-km (27.6-mi) backroad run skirts Bonanza and Ida lakes, a wilderness campsite and several picnic sites.

Access

Drive 21 km (13 mi) north of the Woss cutoff on Highway 19. Cut left onto the gravel road on the south side of the Steele Creek bridge near the Zeballos turn. The route is gravel with hills and sharp corners. Active hauling occurs in some areas. A 4 x 4 may be required on inactive secondary roads.

Description

Near the Zeballos turnoff on Highway 19 there's a logging road on the right side of the highway that winds up to Bonanza Lake and north to Beaver Cove. I had been meaning to venture on this backroad many times before, but never did—until recently, as part of an extended North Island jaunt. All the maps I had (including some recent issues) showed the cutoff starting on the north side of the Steele Creek highway bridge, so that's where I turned. Immediately I was confronted by two rather questionable choices: cross the Cana-

Beaver Cove often bustles with logging activity.

dian Forest Products (Canfor) tracks and take an obviously deteriorated, overgrown spur or head back over Steele Creek on a rail
bridge that also accommodated logging trucks. Problem was, my
vehicle's wheelbase was too narrow for the span. After scouting
around a few minutes, I located a second access, but on the creek's
south side. It was easy enough to find, so I wondered why all the
mapmakers had apparently misplaced the road. I went back onto
Highway 19, zipped over Steele Creek again and swung left onto the
elusive artery to begin a run up the Steele Creek Valley.

In this first part of the route, keep left at any junctions; one is
signposted Markusen Road, to the right. The road crosses a bridge
around the 6-km (3.7-mi) mark and cuts through a region very prone
to slides and washouts. The rock in places is a reddish-brown colour,
similar to ground colouration in areas of northern Ontario. High-
grade copper ore, discovered south of Bonanza Lake in the 1920s,
ignited a temporary mining boom there. The road leaves Canfor
woodlands and enters Fletcher Challenge (FC) territory just south of
Steele Lake, where it is called Branch 80.

Bears often like to ramble down logging roads like those leading to Bonanza Lake, particularly when the berries are ripening. You'll detect the animal's presence by roadside droppings. Sometimes, you'll round a curve and spot a bear, probably already on the move, up ahead. If you're camping in areas where bears are in evidence, remember to be extra careful when storing your food and cooking gear.

The marker for Steele Lake is at km 9.7 (mi 6). I first thought there might be a way down to the lake via spur roads. After checking with the FC Beaver Cove office, I learned there is a road close by, " . . . but it doesn't go right to the lake." Branch 86 swings in on the left (km 11.7/mi 7.3), and at km 13 (mi 8.1) Bonanza Lake appears off in the distance. You can't miss Whistle Corner: its name is blazoned on a sheer rock wall where the road veers east. From a vantage point above Bonanza Lake's south end you can look out onto the lake, the Bonanza River and the nearby Bonanza Range of mountains, dominated by the often snowy heights of Mount Ashwood.

Just over the 14-km (8.7-mi) mark you'll cross the Bonanza River bridge and cut through a logging yard. At km 14.7 (mi 9.1) you'll arrive at the junction with Main Road South, the mainline winding north to Beaver Cove. To the right, in the vicinity of Branch 45, a giant cypress tree will intrigue tree viewers. Turn left and watch for the entrance to the FC wilderness campsite on Bonanza Lake (km 15.4/mi 9.6). It's a short drive into the camping area. If you're travelling in the off-season, you may find the campsite vacant. Then you'll have your choice of ten user-maintained sites, several of them on a small bank overlooking the lake. Two comfort stations are provided, as well as picnic tables, concrete fire pits (some with grates and rings) and garbage cans. At campsites such as this, with limited trash pickup, visitors can help maintain them by always carrying out their trash, whether there are garbage receptacles or not. This prevents any unsightly overflow that could attract scavenging animals.

You can hike along the rough beach at Bonanza Lake down to the Bonanza River mouth. Several wet areas have to be crossed where tiny creeks seep into the lake, so the use of gum boots will keep your feet dry. The reddish gravels of the shoreline give way to fine sand as you near the river mouth. Here, large logs and trees make the hiking somewhat more difficult. You can walk north from the campsite to an abandoned piece of logging machinery near the campsite's boat launch. The ramp has a series of concrete steps to assist the launching of small, trailered boats. Road access is from the mainline, down a short spur just north of the campsite entrance.

The Bonanza Lake run leads travellers along the east side of Bonanza Lake.

Bonanza Lake lies geographically in a north/south position, bordered by the Hankin Range and the Bonanza Range. Prevailing wind patterns are much like those on Nimpkish Lake, further to the east. On most larger Island lakes you'll find the wind is up by late morning, creating tricky boating conditions. The Bonanza Lake campsite is on a relatively unprotected part of the lake, and, with over 5 km (3 mi) of fetch, strong, steady winds create tossing waves and rollers right offshore. Take care out on the water and watch the weather.

Main Road South follows Bonanza Lake's east side. At one point it passes directly below a rock face and fire burn on the steep flank of Whiltilla Mountain. At a junction near Bonanza Lake's top end (km 24.8/mi 15.4) you can turn left and cross the Bonanza River bridge to the old road that dead-ends at a picnic site. Pilings from a booming ground still stand out in the lake. Canoes, kayaks and small cartoppers can easily be launched here. Bonanza Lake has recently been stocked with rainbow trout and also contains Dolly Varden (char), cutthroat trout and kokanee. Late spring and early fall are prime times for fishing.

Travellers planning backroad explorations beyond the picnic-site spur should note that Fletcher Challenge has recently been hauling down Misery Main, just east of Mount Hoy. This is one road on which you don't want to meet a loaded off-road truck coming downhill. Pulloffs and turnarounds are scattered, and there are many narrow stretches and blind corners. It's best to wait until after the loggers are done for the day. Call the FC Beaver Cove office for hauling and access updates prior to your trip. There's an old road on the right, just beyond the picnic-site access, that once snaked around the west side of Ida Lake. This route is now heavily overgrown, with sinkholes and washed-out creek crossings that even deter backwoods browsers with 4 x 4s.

From the km-24.8 (mi-15.4) junction, Main Road South runs north to parallel Ida Lake. Ida Lake is wide at its tip, then it narrows into a sliver of water before opening up a bit at its south end. Ida Lake reminds me of Gray Lake in the Sayward Forest near Campbell River: they both are surrounded by marshy vegetation, and both narrow into river-like channels.

The mainline crosses the Kokish River bridge (km 31.4/mi 19.5) and then parallels the river. At several spots the river churns through rock canyons. By km 41 (mi 25.5) you'll reach the old Kokish logging camp yard and then start down a hill. At km 42.2 (mi 26.2), you'll hit the junction with the paved road out to Highway 19. Turn left here for Campbell River and Port McNeill. Keep straight ahead for Bauza Cove, Beaver Cove and the picturesque village of Telegraph Cove, about 2.5 km (1.6 mi) away.

Beaver Cove was once the northern end of a B.C. Ferry run from Kelsey Bay. That was before the Island Highway was completed in the late 1970s. The ferry service is now discontinued, yet Beaver Cove still bustles with activity. Canfor's Beaver Cove dryland sort is the terminus of one of the last operating logging railways in the world. The line stretches all the way to Vernon Camp. Fletcher Challenge trucks logs to the cove for sorting. Logs are then towed to mainland mills. The FC Beaver Cove logging office is on the way to Telegraph Cove. You can stop in and pick up a copy of their Beaver Cove logging road guide. (Finally, a map that shows the highway turnoff on Steele Creek's south side.) It is also available at the Forestry Infocentre at the junction of Highway 19 and the Beaver Cove road.

Telegraph Cove is nestled on a tiny bay on Johnstone Strait. Most of the village sits on pilings connected by a boardwalk. The historic but idle sawmill started by the pioneering Wastell family is one point of interest. Sport fishing and whale watching (the hamlet is close to Robson Bight) lure countless visitors over the summer.

I stayed an extra day at the Bonanza Lake campsite to take in some sunshine and watch blustery winds whip up whitecaps out in the lake. That evening, as sunset approached, I meandered along the boat-launch road, intending to walk up to the mainline and back to camp down the main entrance. As I neared the campsite spur, a slight movement next to the roadside bushes caught my eye. I stopped and at first thought it was a deer. Wrong. A deer doesn't crouch; cougars do. We stared at each other for a few seconds, then the cat scurried across the road, took a single, graceful leap over a pile of roadside gravel and vanished into the woods. This was not my first encounter with the elusive cougar. I had spotted one once before; ironically, not far from my driveway at home. That time all I got was a glimpse of the cat's hindquarters and tail. Seeing the Bonanza Lake cougar provided my first full look. Perhaps I was the first human it had ever encountered. Whatever the circumstances, we each went off in opposite directions, none the worse for the experience.

Contacts

Fletcher Challenge (Beaver Cove Division) (604) 928-3111/928-3114; Canadian Forest Products (Woss) (604) 281-2300; North Island Forestry Centre (Beaver Cove) (604) 956-3844; B.C. Forest Service (Port McNeill) (604) 956-5000.

Maps/Guides

Fletcher Challenge Beaver Cove Logging Road Guide; Canadian Forest Products Nimpkish Valley Logging Road Guide; B.C. Forest Service Port McNeill Forest District Recreation Map; National Topographical Series: 92L/7 Nimpkish (1:50,000); 92L/10 Alert Bay (1:50,000); Provincial Map: 92L Alert Bay (1:250,000).

Nearest Services

Woss; Nimpkish; Telegraph Cove; Port McNeill.

TRIP 24: Anutz Lake to Nimpkish Lake

In Brief

The Nimpkish Valley has countless destinations for Island adventurers. One paddling favourite is near the south end of Nimpkish Lake. From the wilderness campsite at Anutz Lake, you can journey by canoe to the south end of Nimpkish Lake, close to the mouth of the Nimpkish River.

Access

Take the Zeballos turn on Highway 19 (about 21 km/13 mi north of the Woss cutoff) and follow the signs to the Anutz Lake campsite. The route is combined-use mainlines and secondary roads.

Description

I've stopped in the Nimpkish Valley many times over the years. In the off-season, with limited daylight hours, an overnight stop at Anutz Lake still gives you time for some evening fishing, particularly if you're journeying north from Victoria. A couple of times friends and I have based at Anutz for a few days of canoeing and fishing.

From the cutoff on Highway 19 the Zeballos Road parallels the paved road and then swings left. Cross the Nimpkish River bridge to a signposted fork (km 2.7/mi 1.7). Keep right, toward Zeballos. To the left winds along the south side of the river and eventually back to Woss. At the next junction (3-km/1.9-mi mark), turn off the Zeballos

Having a boat or canoe helps anglers reach more fishing spots. (Photo by Bill Hadden)

Road and follow the Anutz Lake markers. Keep right, approximately 6 km (3.7 mi) in, for Anutz Lake. The left fork continues on to Little Hustan Lake Cave Regional Park, with caves and the interesting rock formations of Atluck Creek.

On the final approach to Anutz Lake the road drops down a small hill and enters a wide clearing where you'll find a choice of camping areas; some close to the lakeside, others nestled in a forested fringe. Canadian Forest Products (Canfor) has provided picnic tables and a boat launch. The site was once a logging camp. In fact, the whole region is steeped in history. In 1862, the first crossing of Vancouver Island by Europeans took place. (See Trip 26.) With the help of native guides, coastal surveyors set out from Kyuquot, journeyed up the Tahsish River to Atluck Lake, over to Hustan and Anutz lakes and down Nimpkish Lake to the Island's east coast. The company followed game trails on land and constructed rafts for the lake and river crossings. How different is travel more than a century later: comfortable cars and trucks follow paved and gravel roads; modern canoes, kayaks and cartop boats powered by outboard motors make our outdoor endeavours seem almost tame when compared to the rigours and hardships endured with primitive equipment by the early adventurers.

Anglers often troll or cast at the Atluck creek mouth or the stream coming in from Diane Lake. In cooler weather the trout tend to be sluggish. Fish sign on the surface may be nonexistent. At times like this, it's best to fish deep—and be patient. Any bites will probably be sporadic. The lake was stocked with rainbow trout in the late 1980s.

One early spring, some friends and I based at Anutz Lake. We had encountered heavy rains on the way up, but as we neared our destination, things let up a bit. Behind a canopy of scudding clouds we caught glimpses of stars as evening approached. With the partial clearing the temperature soon dropped and we were thankful we had brought along a small portable heater.

The next morning dawned grey and drizzly, though it was warming up somewhat. That just might trigger the fish into action. Some locals drove in as we were finishing breakfast. They seemed surprised that anyone would be tenting so early in the year. We were starting to think the same thing. One of them was good enough to suggest a couple of possible hot spots and lure set-ups. He added, "You can spend hours on the water, nothing showing, then—Bang!—the bite's on." (Usually freshwater anglers aren't as talkative as saltwater anglers are concerning local fishing knowledge.)

Soon we were out in the canoe, working the creek mouths, rocky dropoffs and shoreline weed patches. Not much happened in the way of fish—at first. Showers passed over us and it looked like it was going to be a wet day on the water. Then without warning, the bobbers dipped. "Fish on!" went the cry, and as one of us reached for the net, all three of us had strikes. No sooner had we placed the fish on the stringer and sent out our lines again, than another triple strike doubled our catch. We limited out in half an hour or less and proceeded back to camp, elated and surprised. The cutthroat were good-sized and made for an excellent lunch, with plenty left over for supper.

The daily quota for trout at that time was much higher. And even if the catch limit was the same today, we wouldn't keep as many fish. We're selective about what we keep and retain only enough fish for a quick meal; and then, only occasionally. Any other fish brought to the gunwales, particularly the larger ones, are carefully unhooked, revived (if necessary) and released. This policy hones our fish-releasing techniques and hopefully, will safeguard the fishery for future anglers. Many catch-and-release trout fishermen pinch the barbs off their hooks and employ a hemostat to better their fish-release success. This device's slender shape, curved tip and locking handle is a great advantage when dealing with a deeply imbedded hook. You can buy hemostats in medical-supply outlets, outdoor stores and most fly-fishing shops.

Anutz Lake is connected to Nimpkish Lake by a short stream. You can paddle and line your way into Nimpkish Lake's south end. An old logging trestle still stands at the north end of the connecting waterway. The mouth of the Nimpkish River is a little over 1 km (0.6 mi) away. Karmutzen Mountain, the giant of the Karmutzen Range,

The Nimpkish River, seen here east of Woss, can be paddled and portaged all the way to Nimpkish Lake.

stands guard over Nimpkish Lake; Tlakwa Mountain dominates the backdrop further south.

If the lake is calm enough, you can journey along the eastern shore to the tiny community of Nimpkish, north of the river mouth. Many paddlers also journey down the Nimpkish River to Nimpkish Lake. There are a number of access points to the river closer to Woss. (*Whitewater Trips for Kayakers, Canoeists and Rafters on Vancouver Island*, by Betty Pratt-Johnson, details a number of options.) Some river travellers are taking part in one of the wilderness canoeing expeditions offered at Strathcona Park Lodge, the outdoor education centre on Upper Campbell Lake. Their take-out point is the Canfor Nimpkish Lake campsite, just down the hill at Nimpkish. This locale is popular with windsurfers. Each August, surfers from across North America converge here for the annual "Speed Weekend." Strong, daily winds on the lake provide excellent conditions for sailboarding. These same winds can cause problems for paddlers, particularly those with open canoes. Blustery conditions usually develop by mid-morning and last till late afternoon. Local residents say the lake can get so rough that larger boats have problems. There are times when it blows all night, too. If you plan on tackling Nimpkish Lake, keep close to the shore and watch the weather carefully.

Contacts

Canadian Forest Products (Woss) (604) 281-2300; B.C. Forest Service (Port McNeill) (604) 956-5000.

Maps/Guides

Canadian Forest Products Nimpkish Valley Logging Road Guide; B.C. Forest Service Port McNeill Forest District Recreation Map; *Whitewater Trips for Kayakers, Canoeists and Rafters on Vancouver Island* (Pratt-Johnson/Soules/Pacific Search); National Topographical Series: 92L/7 Nimpkish Lake (1:50,000); Provincial Map: 92L Alert Bay (1:250,000).

Nearest Services

Nimpkish; Port McNeill; Woss.

TRIP 25: Backroads: Nimpkish Lake to Tahsish Inlet

In Brief

The logging roads near the south end of Nimpkish Lake can be followed all the way to Tahsish Inlet. From this launch point paddlers can explore the head of the inlet or try a river journey up the Tahsish River. There is a Canadian Forest Products (Canfor) campsite at Atluck Lake and a number of viewpoints on the way.

Access

Take the Zeballos turn on Highway 19 (about 21 km/13 mi) north of Woss. Gravel mainlines (good-to-fair shape) are shared with industrial traffic in some sections; washouts and temporary closures are possible in the off-season. There are some steep hills along the route.

Description

I am always lured by logging roads that go out to the west coast. With continued logging, newer roads are opening up many previously inaccessible regions. One such area is Tahsish Inlet, an inner reach of Kyuquot Sound. Woss-based Canadian Forest Products has been active in the upper Tahsish for a number of years; Fletcher Challenge has operated along the Artlish River. Industrial roads now reach a Fletcher Challenge industrial site on Tahsish Inlet and provide

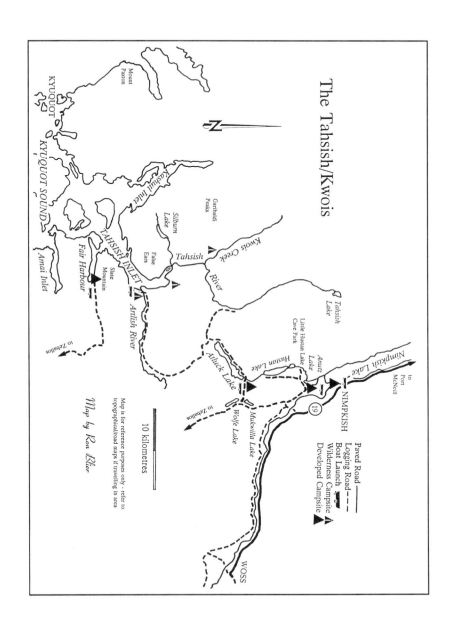

The Tahsish/Kwois

N

Map is for reference purposes only - refer to topographical/road maps if travelling in area

10 kilometres

Map by Ron Bkler

Paved Road ——
Logging Road ---
Boat Launch ⚓
Wilderness Campsite ▲
Developed Campsite ▲

KYUQUOT

KYUQUOT SOUND

Amai Inlet

Fair Harbour

Mount Paxton

Kashutl Inlet

Garibaldi Peaks

Silburn Lake

False Ears

Tahsish

Kwois Creek

Tahsish River

Slate Mountain

TAHSISH INLET

Artlish River

to Zeballos

Attluck Lake

Tahsish Lake

Little Husian Lake Cave Park

Husian Lake

Anutz Lake

Mukwilla Lake

to Zeballos

Wolfe Lake

Nimpkish Lake

NIMPKISH

to Port McNeill

19

WOSS

convenient water access for boaters and paddlers. The route from Highway 19 to the coast follows 47 km (29.2 mi) of Canfor and Fletcher Challenge logging mainlines to the Artlish River mouth.

The many confusing intersections along these backroads are clearly signposted. Take the Zeballos turn on the highway between Port McNeill and Woss and reset your vehicle's trip meter to zero. Just a short way in from the highway, you'll reach a bridge over the Nimpkish River. At km 2.7 (mi 1.7) keep right for Zeballos; a left goes back to Woss and follows the south side of the Nimpkish River. Anglers can reach river pools (with a little bushwacking) from numerous points along this backroad. At km 3 (mi 1.9) keep left for Zeballos. A right here leads to the Canfor campsite at Anutz Lake. Outdoor adventurers use this wilderness campground (once a logging camp) as a base for area angling and backroad explorations. A sloping boat ramp accommodates small, trailered boats. (See Trip 24.)

Stay on the Anutz Lake road to reach Little Hustan Lake Cave Regional Park. Located on Atluck Creek, the stream that connects Atluck Lake with Anutz Lake, the park features caves, rock arches and a natural rock bridge in the Atluck Canyon. There are many such limestone formations on northern Vancouver Island; Little Hustan Cave Regional Park is one of the most accessible.

Cut right at km 9.1 (mi 5.7) onto Atluck Road and follow the signs for Atluck Lake. This route runs between Mukwilla and Wolfe lakes, the latter a good trout fishing destination in the late spring or early fall. A left at the junction leads to Zeballos and further west to Fair Harbour, where a logging camp once stood. It was dismantled in 1969 and relocated at Zeballos. Today Fair Harbour is known as the launch point for Kyuquot, the tiny, mixed native and white community on outer Kyuquot Sound. Saltwater anglers, kayakers and canoeists make this their jumping-off point for Kyuquot Sound waters. Some travellers base at the nearby B.C. Forest Service campsite.

Atluck Lake (km 12.7/mi 7.9) has a Canfor campsite and boat launch on its eastern shore. Pinder Peak's craggy crown is a striking backdrop for spring and fall anglers seeking the lake's rainbow trout. Atluck Lake is narrow in places and bordered by sheer mountains. The wind can come up suddenly to create heavy chop and potentially tricky water conditions for smaller boats. The mainline hugs the cliffs along Atluck's north side to lakehead (km 19/mi 11.8).

A little beyond Welch Main you'll reach a junction (km 20.6/mi 12.8). Atluck Road veers off to the right. Keep left onto Artlish Main. The road climbs a steep switchback. At the Artlish Cutoff (km 24.8/mi

The scars of recent logging are evident on Tahsish Inlet.

15.4) stay left on Artlish Main. You'll pass Apollo Road and then, at km 27.5 (mi 17.1), keep left again on Artlish Main. The spur on the right is East Artlish Main. The route negotiates a blind hairpin corner and runs through stands of old-growth forest occasionally broken by cutblocks.

The Artlish River parallels the mainline most of the way to Tahsish Inlet. Watch for deep pools in the river as the Artlish estuary suddenly opens up before you. Just under the 47-km (29.2-mi) mark you'll reach the gravel boat launch and dock at the Fletcher Challenge log dump. I describe a Tahsish—Kwois paddling adventure in Trip 26.

Contacts

Canadian Forest Products (Woss) (604) 281-2300; Fletcher Challenge (Beaver Cove Division) (604) 928-3111/928-3114; B.C. Forest Service (Port McNeill) (604) 956-5000.

Maps/Guides

Canadian Forest Products Nimpkish Valley Logging Road Guide (depicts logging roads from Highway 19 to Atluck Lake); Canadian Pacific Forest Products (CPFP) Tahsish Pacific Region Map (includes logging roads west of Atluck Lake/See Map Sources); B.C. Forest Service Port McNeill Forest District Recreation Map; National Topographical Series: 92L/2 Woss Lake (1:50,000); 92L/3 Kyuquot (1:50,000); 92L/7 Nimpkish (1:50,000); Provincial Map: 92L Alert Bay (1:250,000).

Nearest Services

Nimpkish; Woss.

TRIP 26: Tahsish—Kwois Paddling Adventure

In Brief

Wilderness canoeing enthusiasts will savour a journey up the Tahsish River to the confluence with Kwois Creek. It's not for beginners. This trip involves sea and river travel with lining and portaging. But a paddle into an untouched wilderness will lure many Island adventurers.

Access

Take the Kyuquot cutoff on Highway 19 and follow Canadian Forest Products and Fletcher Challenge roads to Tahsish Inlet. (See Trip 25.)

Description

Clearcuts, second-growth forests and logging roads cover much of Vancouver Island. Man's modifications scar the mountainsides and river valleys. Even surviving pockets of virgin forest are fast disappearing. One region still exuding an elixir of isolation and timelessness lies at the head of Tahsish Inlet, a coastal indentation on Kyuquot Sound.

People often confuse Tahsish with Tahsis. Both names are derived from the Indian word—"tashee"—meaning trail or path. The west coast community of Tahsis lies at the head of Tahsis Inlet, a narrow reach knifing inland on Nootka Island's east side. The Tahsish region is to the northwest, near Fair Harbour; as the raven flies, it's about 45 km (28 mi) southwest of Port McNeill.

Sections of the Tahsish River are quite shallow.

The Tahsish River estuary is habitat for a profusion of bird, insect, plant, animal and marine life. The Tahsish River is the top salmonid producer on northwest Vancouver Island: its gravels are the spawning grounds for five species of salmon. Cutthroat and rainbow trout are present, along with summer steelhead. With the onset of the fall salmon runs, eagles and black bears throng to the estuary. The lower Tahsish Valley contains critical wintering range for deer and Roosevelt elk. Some trees in the region rival the aging giants of the Carmanah Valley, and include Canada's tallest known western hemlock (75.6 m/248 ft).

The Tahsish area has a rich history. The first recorded crossing of Vancouver Island by a European (in 1862) began at the Tahsish estuary. During a coastal survey under the direction of Captain George H. Richards of HMS *Hecate*, two expedition members (Lieutenant Phillip Hankin and Surgeon-Lieutenant Charles Wood) and a number of native guides twice ventured up the Tahsish Valley. They took the Grease Trail, a Kyuquot trading route to the Nimpkish that followed elk trails. High water and impossible river crossings thwarted the explorers on their initial attempt. A second gruelling trek to the Nimpkish Valley via Atluck, Hustan, Anutz and Nimpkish lakes to Fort Rupert was successful.

You can paddle to the head of Tahsish Inlet and then hike up the Tahsish River floodplain on riparian-zone game trails. Some travellers prefer to paddle and portage their way upriver through a series of large, deep pools to the confluence with Kwois Creek, the Tahsish's primary tributary. Further upstream, steep canyons and boisterous waterfalls geographically sever the unlogged lower Tahsish River Valley and the adjoining Silburn and Kwois watersheds from the already-logged upper Tahsish.

On our Tahsish paddling adventure we arrived at the launch point late in the day. The saltchuck was somewhat agitated, so we set up a wilderness camp where we were and plotted our strategies for an early-morning departure. (The *Canadian Tide and Current Tables: Vol. 6* will help visitors calculate inlet tides.) Next day the contrary winds had died down, leaving inlet waters more conducive to travel. We worked our way across the wide shallows of the Artlish River estuary and then swung toward a range of mountains called False Ears. There are few wilderness camping spots on these shores. We scouted out the bay at the head of Tahsish Inlet and noted one or two possible tent sites, both rather close to the tidal zone. Then it was into the current and up the Tahsish River.

There were two channels. A short distance up the right one, shallow water and a tangle of fallen trees blocked our way. The left channel took us by old trees whose immense roots plunged into the tidal waters of the estuary, conjuring up images of cypress and mangrove swamps. Here, we could no longer see the inlet nor the distant clearcut behind our launch point. There was only the ancient forest and the murmur of the river. It was like stepping back in time. The illusion was occasionally shattered by a floatplane or the rumble from a motorboat somewhere down the inlet. Such intrusions were fleeting and, like the dissipating gossamer jet trails high overhead, soon forgotten.

We were able to go up the Tahsish from its estuary to the north end of the river island that marks the boundary of a 64-ha (158-ac) ecological reserve. There a barrier of river-churned gravel stopped our progress. We lugged our gear over to the main river channel and set up camp near the mouth of Silburn Creek. The tide backs up the Tahsish River for quite a distance, a fact we took into careful consideration when pitching our tent. River travellers should note that the Tahsish River and Kwois Creek floodplains are extremely unstable and subject to flash flooding. Most of the river valley floor is under water during wet weather.

That evening, on a high tide, we paddled back to the estuary and

Knowledge of tidal camping is essential in the Tahsish-Kwois.

spent a couple of hours gliding through flooded channels and back-waters that were too shallow to negotiate at any other time. Seals sometimes poked their heads up as they foraged inlet waters near the river mouth. Giant cedar, fir and hemlock, many centuries old, fringed the riverbanks.

The next morning we set out for an upriver journey. There was less portaging than we expected, but it didn't take long before our feet were wet from lining and pushing the canoe around gravel bars and through rocky channels. Experienced river travellers anticipate soggy feet; some paddlers wear neoprene booties. It was, unfortunately, an ideal day for biting flies—no wind, clear skies and very hot. We grew accustomed to the sporadic bouts with the flying fiends, and gave particular attention to our encounters with "old green eyes"—the horsefly.

We paused at a river twist, where the swerve of the river had cre-ated an immense jade pool with a lazy back eddy and swarms of bugs flitting just above its surface: a perfect fly-fishing setting when afternoon shadows crept across a corner of the river bend. A three-hour paddle took us from tidewater to the Tahsish-Kwois river junction, where a pro-posed ecological reserve will protect a stand of towering Sitka spruce.

On our downstream run, strong, gusty winds blowing upriver forced us back to steady paddling. (So much for an easy return to the estuary.) We had felt like intruders on our first day on the Tahsish, but we quickly slipped into a low-impact camping mode: the few fires we built were well below the high-tide mark and we painstakingly erased any sign of our campsites before we left. Over our two remaining days, we based at the head of Tahsish Inlet, exploring and watching eagles, seals and a pair of loons that passed by surprisingly close to camp.

In January 1992, the NDP government announced an eighteen-month logging deferral in five contentious regions on Vancouver Island, including the Tahsish—Kwois. Logging in these forests was transferred to less-sensitive areas. What happens at the end of the logging postponement will be clearer by mid-1993. The fact remains that road construction and logging could dramatically change the floodplains, threatening river pools and fish habitat. Roads introduced near prime elk and deer wintering ranges would give poachers easy access. Integrated resource plans are nonetheless vast improvements over previous forest-industry practices.

When the first tree falls to the droning chainsaws, the feral quality of the lower Tahsish-Kwois will be forever lost. It may be unrealistic to expect complete preservation of every untouched watershed on the B.C. coast, but if a pristine treasure like the lower Tahsish-Kwois is not worth saving, what is?

Contacts

Canadian Forest Products (Woss) (604) 281-2300; Fletcher Challenge (Beaver Cove Division) (604) 928-3111/928-3114; B.C. Forest Service (Port McNeill) (604) 956-5000.

Maps/Guides

Canadian Forest Products Nimpkish Valley Logging Road Guide; Canadian Pacific Forest Products Tahsish Pacific Region Map (See Map Sources); B.C. Forest Service Port McNeill Forest District Recreation Map; Canadian Tide and Current Tables: Vol. 6 (Canadian Hydrographic Service); National Topographical Series: 92L/3 Kyuquot (1:50,000); Provincial Map: 92L Alert Bay (1:250,000).

Nearest Services

Woss; Nimpkish; Port McNeill.

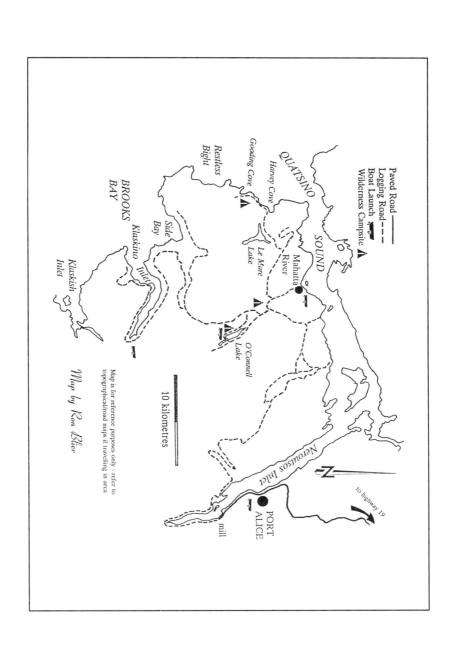

Paved Road ——
Logging Road ----
Boat Launch
Wilderness Campsite ▲

QUATSINO

Restless
Bight

Gooding Cove

Harvey Cove

SOUND

BROOKS
BAY

Side
Bay

Le Mare
Lake

Mahatta
River

Klaskino
Inlet

Klaskish
Inlet

O'Connell
Lake

10 kilometres

Nerousos Inlet

Map is for reference purposes only - refer to
topographical/road maps if travelling in area

Map by Ron Bloe

N

to highway 19

PORT
ALICE

mill

TRIP 27: Backroads to Klaskino Inlet

In Brief

In 1985, a logging road was punched through that linked the networks of Mahatta River-area backroads with Port Alice. The Western Forest Products (WFP) logging community of Mahatta River has since been dismantled, but road building and clearcutting in the area continues. This trip follows remote backroads to several panoramic seascapes on Quatsino Sound and Brooks Bay. Klaskino Main leads ocean kayakers and experienced canoeists to a boat launch at the head of Klaskino Inlet.

Access

Drive to Port Alice and continue south to the pulp mill. The gravel mainline starts near the mill's parking lot. Most main roads are in good shape. There are several long, steep, switchbacking hills. Secondary routes are good to fair, and some require a truck or 4 x 4. Active hauling occurs on many routes. At such times, public access is restricted between 6:00 a.m. and 6:00 p.m. (Monday to Friday).

Description

I first travelled the Mahatta River-area backroads in 1986. A road link to Port Alice had been completed the year before, and when I heard about it, the opportunity to investigate freshwater lakes and rugged coastal logging roads was too intriguing to ignore. Back then, the once-

The rugged shoreface below Mount Bury at Harvey Cove is one example of the savage beauty of the north Island.

isolated logging community of Mahatta River, complete with company swimming pool, sat next to a bay on Quatsino Sound. Less than a decade later you wouldn't even know what the town looked like. All the buildings are gone; the pool has been filled in and only a clearing in the forest marks the former townsite.

Access restrictions play a key part in Island adventuring. Active hauling often involves the wide, off-road logging trucks and although the mainlines are in good shape, they can be narrow and twisty with many blind corners. At such times Western Forest Products limits public entry between 6:00 a.m. and 6:00 p.m. Monday to Friday. Before you tackle these logging roads, stop in at WFP's Jeune Landing office on Quarry Main, just north of Port Alice, and pick up an updated copy of their logging road guide. This recreation map is also available from WFP's Port McNeill office and the Forestry Infocentre at the Beaver Cove turn on Highway 19. Employees can update area fire closures, point out any locked gates and indicate roads on which to exercise extra caution—you might be sharing the mainlines with industrial traffic.

We will begin our jaunt to Klaskino Inlet at the Port Alice mill. Reset your vehicle's trip meter to zero at the start of the gravel. The mainline, called Marine Drive, swings around the head of Neroutsos Inlet and turns north, close to the Colonial Creek salmon hatchery. In 1990, nearby Cayeghle Creek was the site of a habitat-improvement project. The creek's side channels were dug out and restored, creating winter habitat for coho salmon. At km 23.5 (mi 14.6) WFP's Neroutsos Inlet Lookout and Recreation Area looks out over the inlet and Port Alice. This viewpoint is about halfway up the lengthy grade in the Teeta Creek Valley. The mainlines in this area are well marked. Watch for the signposts and keep left onto K Main, I Main, then J Main, near Kewquodie Creek (*Island Adventures*: Trip 33.)

Around the 52.5-km (32.6-mi) mark is a major intersection called The Crossroads. Here the road suddenly widens into a double-wide artery divided by a big ditch. Straight ahead on Mahatta Main is WFP's Mahatta River wilderness campsite (km 53/mi 32.9), co-managed with the B.C. Forest Service (BCFS). This small, scenic campsite on the banks of the Mahatta River has ten user-maintained sites, although several closest to the river have been closed. Erosion from high water has severely undercut the riverbank on which these sites are perched. At this central location many visitors set up a base camp and daytrip on area backroads. I've overnighted here a couple of times. I had a surprise one morning, when I spotted a deer swimming across the river.

At km 54 (mi 33.5) Restless Main angles in on the left; Mahatta Main runs north for 4 km (2.5 mi) to end at the former Mahatta River townsite. You can follow Restless Main about 16 km (9.9 mi) to the seascapes of outer Quatsino Sound. Those at Harvey Cove are superb. Gooding Cove features a picnic site fronting a wild, surf-pounded beach. The route in skirts high above Le Mare Lake and then cuts west at Culleet Creek. Vast clearcuts stretch from the mountaintops right down to lakeside. It's not a pretty sight. Slope stability is a concern in the area: heavy rains a few years ago caused a slide that tumbled right into Le Mare Lake. Similar problems have developed on Red Stripe Mountain near Klaskino Inlet. The logging currently underway in the region is carried out by small contractors. Timber licenses are held by Interfor, Canadian Forest Products and MacMillan Bloedel.

Let's return to The Crossroads and resume our journey to Klaskino Inlet. Cut onto B Main and reset your trip meter to zero. B Main, regularly a hauling road, accesses M Main and B11, the backroads extending down both sides of O'Connell Lake. There is a picnic site with tables, a comfort station, natural boat launch and dock on the east side of the lake, close to a blocked bridge. Backwoods browsers venturing on the older roads in this vicinity will find some of them overgrown and rough. It helps to have a 4 x 4 and good navigation skills.

B Main becomes North Main in the Buck Creek watershed. A little over 10 km (6.2 mi) from The Crossroads is the Klaskino Main cutoff. Turn left and drive through the clearcuts to the open ocean,

Klaskino Inlet can be explored with a kayak.

near Side Bay. The mainline is narrow in spots, and there are many hills. You may encounter sharp rocks and gravel ridges. The route bends south to the mouth of Klaskino Inlet and then parallels the fjord to its east end. Countless submerged reefs and jagged rocks mark the entrance. East of Red Stripe Mountain, the road curves by a striking view looking toward the head of Klaskino Inlet. At km 32.3 (mi 20.1) a gravel boat launch slopes down into the inlet. Sea kayakers and seasoned canoeists are familiar with this water access. Many paddlers launch here for adventures in Klaskino Inlet and Brooks Bay.

You can stay on North Main and swing inland up the Keith River Valley. Cross the bridge and continue another 4 km (2.5 mi) or so for views of Side Bay, the mouth of Klaskino Inlet and, off in the distance, the looming presence of Brooks Peninsula. On the west side of the Keith River bridge, a secondary road, 11.5 km (7.1 mi) in length and accessible by 4 x 4, goes to Le Mare Lake. This route eventually hooks into Restless Main. This backroad can be rough on your vehicle's tires, brakes and cooling system—one grade is a twisting 3 km (1.9 mi) long. Your nerves may not fare any better as you'll encounter confusing side roads, steep hills, loose gravel, sharp rocks, cliffs, switchbacks and flagged sinkholes—the very stuff off-roaders relish.

The logging roads do give travellers access to previously remote areas. But one only has to look at the pre-logging aerial photo in Don Watmough's *West Coast of Vancouver Island* to realize the indelible mark industry has left at Klaskino Inlet. Cutblocks now run right around the lower slopes of the inlet. On Yaky Kop Cone, the big hump facing the inlet's Scouler Pass, there appears to be no logging; at least on the mountain's seaward side. Looks are deceiving. Its back side reflects heavy cutting. Roads are now working their way closer to Brooks Peninsula.

The Klaskish watershed, just south of Klaskino Inlet, is relatively untouched by logging, save for a few spurs dating back to the early 1970s, near a former camp on the estuary. In 1990, a 132-ha (326-ac) ecological reserve was created on the lower Klaskish River and estuary. A logging road has been extended through to a height of land on Klaskish Inlet's north side. On the Kyuquot side of the peninsula (Checleset Bay) logging has already occurred near Ououkinsh Inlet and Malksope Inlet, but not at Nasparti Inlet, west of Mount Seaton. Sitka spruce of record-size width have been discovered in the Nasparti region.

It seems that most of the attention drawn to contentious unlogged regions on the Island focuses in the south, to areas like the Carmanah and Walbran valleys. Of ninety primary watersheds over 5000 ha (12,355 ac) on Vancouver Island, just one, the Moyeha in Strathcona Park, has protected status. And only five pristine watersheds of that size still exist; the rest have been logged, at least partially. For the Klaskish and Nasparti regions, time may be running out.

Contacts

Western Forest Products (Jeune Landing) (604) 284-3395; Western Forest Products (Port McNeill) (604) 956-3391; B.C. Forest Service (Port McNeill) (604) 956-5000.

Maps/Guides

Western Forest Products Visitors' Guide to Northern Vancouver Island; MacMillan Bloedel Port McNeill/Port Hardy Recreation and Logging Road Guide; B.C. Forest Service Port McNeill Forest District Recreation Map; National Topographical Series: 92L/5 Mahatta Creek (1:50,000); 92L/6 Alice Lake (1:50,000); Provincial Map: 92L Alert Bay (1:250,000).

Nearest Services

Port Alice.

TRIP 28: Backroads to Koprino Harbour

In Brief

Not many people are familiar with Koprino Harbour, a large bay on Quatsino Sound. Western Forest Products (WFP) and the residents of Holberg have constructed a beautiful wilderness campsite here at Spencer Cove. This locale is relatively close to Holberg and is an excellent destination for backwoods browsers, scenery seekers and paddlers.

Access

From Port Hardy, take the Holberg Road 45 km (27.9 mi) to Holberg. Cut left onto South Main and follow the signposts to Koprino Harbour. The route follows gravel mainlines. Restricted-access roads may be encountered west of Koprino Harbour.

Description

Usually when I travel the backroads west of Port Hardy, I'm heading to one of the trailheads in Cape Scott Provincial Park. That all changed a few months ago when, instead of hiking, my trip was geared towards backroad exploration of North Island locales I hadn't yet seen. I am always intrigued by destinations by the sea, so the decision was made to add the Western Forest Products wilderness campsite at Koprino Harbour to the itinerary.

For those not familiar with this neck of the Island, Koprino Harbour is a large bay on Quatsino Sound; a fjord-like reach that almost sev-

Koprino Harbour is a picturesque bay in Quatsino Sound.

ers the North Island in two. Koprino Harbour is on this ocean inlet's north side, about halfway between Cape Parkins and Drake Island. You can get there by water from launch points such as Mahatta River, Coal Harbour or Port Alice. Many backwoods browsers prefer to drive in on gravel roads. Starting in Port Hardy, it's 45 km (27.9 mi) to Holberg; from here networks of WFP mainlines snake a further 33 km (20.5 mi) to Koprino Harbour, leading visitors through the mountains north of Ahwhichaolto Inlet.

If you've ever visited Cape Scott Provincial Park, you're familiar with part of the route (*Island Adventures*: Trip 34). Set your vehicle's trip meter to zero at the Cape Scott cutoff on Highway 19, about 2 km (1.2 mi) south of Port Hardy. At km 7 (mi 4.3), you'll hit the Georgie Lake turnoff. There is a B.C. Forest Service (BCFS) wilderness campsite and boat launch on Georgie Lake's east shore. Kains Lake (km 13.5/mi 8.4) will appear on the right. I've had success casting for cutthroat trout from the natural boat ramp.

Next comes Nahwitti Lake. The BCFS has established a natural boat ramp here and their Helper Creek recreation site makes a good stopover. There's room for a handful of small camper units at this user-maintained campsite nestled in a stately grove of balsam. Watch for the entrance at km 27.7 (mi 17.2). The first section of the route follows a Forest Service road to Nahwitti Lake; beyond the lake, you'll be on WFP roads. Obey all posted signs. The road drops to tidewater at Holberg (km 44.8/mi 27.8). In the 1940s, the world's largest floating logging camp stretched along Holberg Inlet. It was only in the next decade that more permanent residences were constructed on the shore.

At the signposted turn for Winter Harbour (km 45.7/mi 28.4), reset your vehicle's trip meter to zero. Cut left onto South Main. This mainline runs by a log sort and around the head of Holberg Inlet to a T-junction. San Josef Main is to the right; keep left on South Main. When a fellow outdoorsman and I drove through this area one late January, road repairs were still ongoing where the logging road parallels the inlet. Deluging rainfall had washed-out many sections. The route hugs the inlet, almost to Pegattem Creek, before veering inland for Winter Harbour. At km 3.6 (mi 2.2) you'll reach the signposted junction with Lake Main. Keep straight ahead for Koprino Harbour and the wilderness campsite. We passed by one area where trees had tumbled down a mud-slick slope onto the roadway. The fallen limbs had already been chainsawed and lay piled by the roadside.

At km 5.1 (mi 3.2) Southeast Main swings off to the right. Lake Main is straight ahead. Keep right and stay on Southeast Main. This artery becomes Koprino Main and follows the Koprino River Valley to the saltchuck at Spencer Cove. The road runs through replanted forests, some dating from the 1970s, others as far back as the 1930s. There is a sharp contrast between the older stands of regrowing trees and those with a relatively shorter lifespan.

In some regions fresh clearcuts are evident on the mountainsides. Heavy equipment, such as grapple yarders, may be visible in the active logging areas. An inspiring vista of Quatsino Sound unfolds at km 21.8 (mi 13.5). The road first curves through a recent cutblock. Then—quite suddenly—the breathtaking panorama unfolds. You can gaze out over Drake Island in Quatsino Sound and beyond to jagged peaks of the various mountain ranges making up the backbone of Vancouver Island. On our exploration we benefitted from several exceptionally haze-free days.

Hathaway Main is on the left at km 24.2 (mi 15). Shortly after passing this junction, we got our first taste of several extremely muddy sections of roadway. By km 28 (mi 17.4) the route parallels the Koprino River. On the right-hand side of the road, intermittently spaced, are sheer rock walls. Simpson Main meets Koprino Main at km 30.4 (mi 18.9). It was in this area we passed a number of off-road haulers parked at roadside. Even when idle, fully loaded logging trucks appear formidable. During active hauling, the loggers manipulating the ponderous vehicles remain in close contact via radio dispatches. This procedure pinpoints just who pulls over and when. You'll see many signposted radio checkpoints on Island backroads.

As you reach sea level, the tidal flats of Koprino Harbour can be

Off-season backwoods browsers often hit the snow line at higher elevations.

seen through the trees. The foreshore is impressive at low tide. The waters of Koprino Harbour shoal quickly. Boaters mooring in this area had best be prepared for deep anchorages. Koprino Harbour, with its many coves and islets, is an excellent paddling destination. Its waters are semi-protected from swell and sudden winds. Canoeists and kayakers should always keep an eye out on the weather. Marine conditions can change abruptly.

At Robson Cove there is a log-booming area and private boat dock. It was here we again had to negotiate a muddy stretch. The road had been churned into a thick ooze from considerable logging-truck traffic. The road then angled away from the water, and we began to wonder if we'd missed the campsite entrance. At times like these the driver has an edge on things—having to watch out for straggler logging trucks, monitor the trip meter and pinpoint crucial junctions, he has no time to look at maps. If an error in navigation has been committed, it's obviously the passenger's fault.

"Well?"

"Well what!" came the terse reply. Things were getting rough.

A sign up ahead indicated an active logging area; another warned of herbicide spraying along the roadside. We stopped at a locked gate. Here the road split into Botel and McNiffe mainlines. We had gone by an old side road a little before the gate. After a quick perusal of our maps, we turned around and went back to the secondary road at km 33.1 (mi 20.6). That obscure spur road is indeed the entrance to the Koprino campsite, although it was unmarked along the mainline when we were there. A sign, closer to the primitive camping area, recognizes the efforts of Holberg and San Josef residents in creating this WFP site.

Wood for campfires is usually provided. Rustic picnic tables complement a limited number of sites fronting the spectacular shores of Spencer Cove. Privacy is a bit of a luxury at the Koprino campsite; it fills up quickly over the warmer months. During the off-season you may discover the site deserted. With log-sorting operations nearby, even then it can be a busy place. Across the bay we could see another set of booms. The drone of a generator drifted over the still waters from an unseen logging site on Botel Main. An inquisitive seal poked its head up to investigate our suppertime clattering, and then dipped out of sight once more to resume its shoreline foraging.

Island adventurers should ensure they have WFP's Visitors' Guide to Northern Vancouver Island at the ready for use in conjunction with area topographical charts. The latter are notorious for not being quite up-to-date. In Victoria the National Topographical Series (scale 1:50,000) can be ordered through Island Blueprint; Earth Quest Books stocks a complete inventory of Vancouver Island charts. (See Map Sources.)

If you live in Victoria, it's a long way to Koprino Harbour: 500 km (310 mi) of paved road; 78 km (48.4 mi) of gravel backroads. And though my first visit was short, it remains a highlight of one of my North Island runs.

Contacts

Western Forest Products (Holberg) (604) 228-3362; B.C. Forest Service (Port McNeill) (604) 956-5000.

Maps/Guides

Western Forest Products Visitors' Guide to Northern Vancouver Island; B.C. Forest Service Port McNeill Forest District Recreation Map; National Topographical Series: 92L/12 Quatsino (1:50,000); 102I/9 San Josef (1:50,000); Provincial Map: 92L Alert Bay (1:125,000).

Nearest Services

Holberg; Winter Harbour.

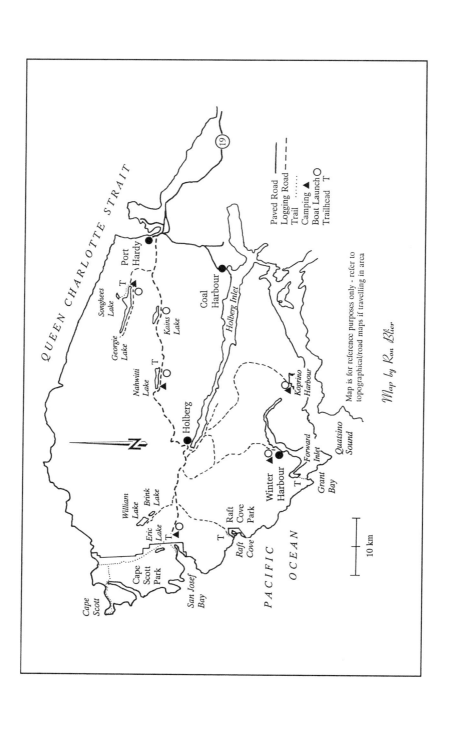

QUEEN CHARLOTTE STRAIT

Port
Hardy

Songhees
Lake   T

Georgie
Lake

Kains
Lake

Nahwitti
Lake   T

Holberg

Coal
Harbour

Holberg Inlet

Koprino
Harbour

Quatsino
Sound

Forward
Inlet

Winter
Harbour

Grant
Bay

William
Lake

Brink
Lake

Eric
Lake   T

Cape
Scott
Park

Raft
Cove
Park

Raft
Cove   T

San Josef
Bay

Cape
Scott

PACIFIC

OCEAN

N

10 km

Paved Road ——
Logging Road — —
Trail ....
Camping ▲
Boat Launch ○
Trailhead T

Map is for reference purposes only - refer to
topographical/road maps if travelling in area

Map by Ron Blier

TRIP 29: Backroads to Winter Harbour

In Brief

Winter Harbour, a tiny coastal community only 26 km (16.1 mi) from Holberg, has its own unique charm. There are hiking trails, a regional campsite and intriguing backroads nearby.

Access

Starting in Holberg, west of Port Hardy, follow South Main to Winter Harbour. An alternate route along SJ 40 starts on San Josef Main and hooks into South Main. Some area mainlines are active hauling roads. The route is winding, with blind corners. Gravel mainlines are in good-to-fair shape.

Description

The majority of North Island visitors travelling the backroads beyond Holberg are heading to the trailheads in Cape Scott and Raft Cove provincial parks. I fell into that habit for a number of years, until the tail end of one trip, when a fellow outdoorsman and I zipped down to Winter Harbour for a quick look. It was on my second visit that I stayed at the local campsite and spent some time exploring the region.

This run starts in Holberg, about 46 km (28.6 mi) from Port Hardy. Turn onto the Western Forest Products (WFP) South Main, near the Scarlet Ibis pub, and reset your vehicle's trip meter to zero. The road cuts through the Holberg logging yard, crosses Goodspeed

There is a BCFS wilderness campsite at Nahwitti Lake.

River to the junction with San Josef Main (km 1/mi 0.6). Keep left on South Main. The mainline parallels Holberg Inlet and skirts a log dump to a fork (km 3.6/mi 2.2). Here you'll swing right, up the Pegattem Creek Valley, to encounter the steepest hill of the run. Straight ahead is Southeast Main and the backroad network to the wilderness campsite at Koprino Harbour. (See Trip 28.)

Most roads in the region are combined-use arteries, with some used more frequently than others by industrial traffic. The Winter Harbour Road is narrow in places, with limited pulloffs. Check ahead with the WFP Holberg office for hauling updates. Many people are inclined to travel after hours on the active hauling roads. To the east of Mount Brandes you'll reach SJ 40 coming in on the right (km 10.9/mi 6.8). This secondary route is an alternate road to and from Winter Harbour. It swings 9 km (5.6 mi) up to San Josef Main. The south section is in better shape and more heavily travelled. From the junction it's just over 5 km (3.1 mi) to the intersection with the DND road that leads to the now-closed CFS Holberg station. The last 4 km (2.5 mi) of SJ 40 are rougher and more overgrown.

South Main continues south. Keep straight ahead at km 21.2 (mi 13.2); to the left is a private road to W.D. Moore Logging. At km 21.9

(mi 13.6) the West Main truck road crosses the mainline. You can loop through the woodlands south of the Macjack River along Top-knot and ML mainlines, but note that active logging in this area may restrict public access. A WFP employee warned me about several spurs shown on the WFP logging road map that are impassable due to deteriorated bridges. Some of the loggers have been in touch with the Ministry of the Environment, promoting trout stocking in one of the area's unnamed lakes.

West Main runs through the Kwalteo Creek Valley and accesses the spur road leading to the trailhead to Grant Bay, a wild beach close to Cape Parkins. WFP employees cleared the trail early in 1992, making it a little easier to hook up with the mud flats of Browning Inlet, but it's still an arduous route, so go prepared. Slippery log crossings and muddy sections are sometimes unavoidable. The trail then skirts the flats to the south end of the inlet. Here the trail again enters the forest, and is more pronounced, as many people boat or paddle in from Winter Harbour. If you time the tide right, you can start your trek close to the more travelled trailhead. Hiking Trails III, published by the Outdoor Club of Victoria Trails Information Society, has a chapter on the Grant Bay Trail.

On its final approach to Winter Harbour, the road dips and dives over hilly terrain. Watch for the totem pole at the entrance to the Kwaksistah campground, on the left, about 1 km (0.6 mi) from the town. Operated by the Regional District of Mount Waddington (Port McNeill), this picturesque campsite is an excellent spot to base for area exploration—and there's no fee. The campsite has fire pits, pic-nic tables and a covered barbeque pit. Some of the campsites even have wooden tent platforms. The adjacent boat launch is best used at high tide. Space is limited at this twelve-site locale, particularly over the summer. In the off-season it's less crowded.

When I based there in early June, a crew from Port McNeill was cleaning up the site for the upcoming season. They seemed sur-prised to discover tenters there at that time of the year. When the sun goes down, you can look south from the Kwaksistah campsite to Winter Harbour and Greenwood Point to see the village lights re-flected on the waters. On a still night you can hear the hum from the fish plant.

Forward Inlet, one of Quatsino Sound's northern reaches, con-stricts at Greenwood Point and then widens out to become Winter Harbour. The fishing and logging town of the same name straddles the shoreline north of the point. The area's protected waters are a

The tiny North Island community of Winter Harbour is close to the Kwaksistah campsite.

haven for commercial fishermen waiting out Pacific storms. The waterway narrows east of Wedel Island and broadens again as Ahwhichaolto Inlet. Seasoned paddlers often prefer regions where logging roads have yet to intrude. For now Ahwhichaolta Inlet remains one possible choice; but logging roads are creeping in from the Koprino Harbour area.

Winter Harbour's waterfront features a wooden boardwalk, harkening back to the days when the hamlet could only be reached by water. Gravel roads were punched through in the 1970s. Telephone and hydro lines reached the community just a few years ago. Stop in at the general store. You can't miss it: it's the big, square building at the end of the road. They sell everything from groceries to marine supplies. The majority of the customers are fishermen, boaters and visiting yachtsmen.

The trailhead at Botel Park is on the right at km 25.9 (mi 16.1). Look for wooden stairs next to a tiny parking area. The trail winds through majestic old growth to the beachfront on Forward Inlet. Remember to time your hike for low tide. (Information on area tides is available in the *Canadian Tide and Current Tables: Vol. 6*, published by the Canadian Hydrographic Service.) Some people are content to stop at the picnic table overlooking the inlet. From here you can watch for eagles or take in a seemingly constant parade of boats coming from and going to Winter Harbour. Once on the beach you can walk west to a spectacular view looking out toward Quatsino Sound. Most of the beach is comprised of stone, so you have to pick your steps carefully. You might spot a bear foraging for berries in shoreline bushes. There is a small patch of sand at the far end of the beach where some visitors carry in picnic lunches. The rocks start just beyond a bubbling creek that enters the saltwater as a mini-falls. Intrepid hikers can scramble up and around the rocks, where on a clear day you can make out mountain landmarks at the mouth of Quatsino Sound; looming in the distance is Brooks Peninsula, a finger of rolling hills jutting out into the Pacific Ocean.

On a future North Island jaunt I'll be bringing my canoe. The paddle from Winter Harbour to Browning Inlet is too alluring to miss. And maybe, if the weather permits, there will be time for a day or two at Ahwhichaolta Inlet as well.

Contacts

Western Forest Products (Holberg) (604) 228-3362; B.C. Forest Service (Port McNeill) (604) 956-5000.

Maps/Guides

Western Forest Products Visitors' Guide to Northern Vancouver Island; B.C. Forest Service Port McNeill Forest District Recreation Map; Canadian Tide and Current Tables: Vol. 6 (Canadian Hydrographic Service); Hiking Trails III (Outdoor Club of Victoria Trails Information Society); National Topographical Series: 92L/12 Quatsino (1:50,000); 102I/8 Cape Parkins (1:50,000); 102I/9 San Josef (1:50,000); Provincial Map: 92L Alert Bay (1:250,000).

Nearest Services

Winter Harbour; Holberg.

TRIP 30: Raft Cove Provincial Park

In Brief

Raft Cove Provincial Park features a wild, west coast beach close to the mouth of the Macjack River. It's a great hiking destination if you like raw wilderness and stunning seascapes. Determined hikers carry a backpack along the challenging trail to the beach and set up a wilderness camp facing the open Pacific.

Access

From Holberg, follow the signs west to Ronning Main, about 12 km (7.5 mi) away. From Ronning Main, follow Branch RN700 to its end at the parking area at the Raft Cove trailhead. Ronning and San Josef mainlines are active hauling roads. Be prepared to back up to roadside pull-outs to avoid off-road logging trucks on weekdays. The mainlines are in good shape; secondary roads are good to fair.

Description

The weather didn't co-operate on my first visit to Raft Cove. In fact, it was downright miserable. Systems surged in from the Pacific with high winds and deluging showers. There were some lulls though, and Ron and I hoped for an extended break in conditions. We were all too familiar with the wind-driven rains that can pelt the Cape Scott area, so we had prepared for a soggy beach foray. Full raingear went on, then our day packs. Our first taste of the Raft Cove Trail was a

A *makeshift raft sits on the beach near the mouth of the Macjack River.*

creek crossing. It required careful balancing on a slick log and precise manipulation of a hand rope lashed to streamside trees. Then it
was up and down a mud-slick footpath that cut around, on, and
sometimes through giant trees, centuries old. Showers persisted, and
by the time we hit the beach, the wind and surf were really thunder-
ing. We set up a tarp shelter near the mouth of the Macjack River
and watched the river current battle incoming swells. After several
hours of wild, west coast atmosphere, we returned to our overnight
shelter, a small camperette. The storms didn't let up much. We were
lashed by gale force winds and rain all night.

Holberg residents and area loggers knew of Raft Cove long before the region became a provincial park. A trail was flagged through
from a branch road in a 1984 cutblock along Ronning Creek. Caulked
boots were essential on this route, which traversed deadfall, boglands
and severe mudholes. When you finally reached the Macjack River,
there were two options: locate an old canoe and negotiate the river
to the beach; or wait for low tide and hike down the Macjack—with
two river crossings to make as well.

Western Forest Products (WFP) extended Ronning Main further
west and newer Raft Cove trails were cut through. One parallelled
Graham Creek to the rocks on the beach's north end. A second route
at the end of RN700 was also ribboned and cleared. This is now the

designated park trail to Raft Cove Provincial Park. Established in 1990, the park includes 405 ha (1000 ac) of forest donated by Western Forest Products. Raft Cove is situated just below San Josef Bay, part of Cape Scott Provincial Park. (*Island Adventures*: Trip 35.) The rocky headlands of Cape Palmerston are to the north. To the south is the rugged isthmus of Commerell Point. In between lies the beautiful, yet exposed sandy beach and the estuary of the Macjack River.

To reach the Raft Cove trailhead, you first drive the 46 km (28.5 mi) or so from Port Hardy to Holberg. Continue west another 12 km (7.5 mi) to the intersection of San Josef Main and Ronning Main. (*Island Adventures*: Trip 34.) Reset your vehicle's trip meter to zero and take Ronning Main through clearcuts and patches of old growth to Branch R700 (km 10.2/mi 6.3). Cut left and drive to the very end of the road. You can park at the trailhead or on an adjacent spur that stops on an exposed hill.

The 1-km (0.6-mi) trail begins at the bottom of a steep bank, close to a creek crossing. There was a plank bridge in place a few years ago, but it was washed away. A sloping log with a hand rope now suffices. The trail winds through an unlogged coastal forest consisting mainly of hemlock, Sitka spruce and western red cedar. Muddy sections are common, and you'll encounter slippery log crossings and blowdowns. Several hills surround Raft Cove and the trail snakes up and down the flank of one of them. Depending on weather conditions, the amount of gear you bring and your hiking pace, you should reach the beach in about forty-five minutes or less.

Many visitors day-hike to the beach, but others carry in overnight gear. One feature of Raft Cove is its forested beach spit. On one side is the Pacific; on the other is the Macjack River. You can camp up on the beach when tides are low enough, or locate the wilderness campsites in the woods at the end of the spit. There's a tiny stream on the beach's north end, but the best water supply is on the south side of the Macjack. You'll have to wait for low tide and wade over the river on its firm sand bottom. Be prepared to get your feet and legs wet in the attempt. The last time I visited Raft Cove, there was a raft constructed out of flotsam and styrofoam floats that could be used in the crossing. Make sure you have accurate tidal information, available in the *Canadian Tide and Current Tables: Vol. 6*, published by the Canadian Hydrographic Service. You wouldn't want to be trapped by a high tide should you decide to explore the rocky shoreline near Commerell Point.

Some hikers are content to walk along Raft Cove's spectacular

Just visible through the trees, an old trapper's cabin still stands near the mouth of the Macjack River.

beach. At low tide you can scramble over the rocks at the north end where the sea has cut an arch in the rugged shoreline. Also at low tide you can venture up the river a fair distance on the exposed river bottom. If you're lucky, you may see a black bear foraging in the tide zone. Look for cougar and wolf tracks as well. Eagles are a common sight. A friend and I once saw one wheel over the beach to suddenly be joined by a second bird that flew up from the spit's tree line.

Raft Cove was first settled by early pioneers of the Cape Scott region. The Boytle family and Willie Hecht arrived in 1913. A trail extended along the coast from Raft Cove up to Cape Palmerston and northeast to the San Josef Bay. A second footpath ran east to join the San Josef wagon road near the Ronning settlement. The colonizing efforts slowly failed, and the majority of settlers moved on. Willie Hecht eventually relocated at Holberg. The passage of time obliterated most of the old trails and homesteads, but Willie Hecht's old trapping cabin still stands on the south side of the Macjack River. (*The Cape Scott Story*, by Lester R. Petersen, is a must-read for those interested in the history of the Cape Scott area.)

You might think, by looking at the area topographical map and WFP's logging road guide, that the Macjack River can be accessed from a logging road, north of Topknot Lake, and then paddled to its mouth. What the maps don't show you are the many fallen trees and huge logs jamming the waterway. A WFP employee from Holberg told me he scouted out possible launching points in the area last year. "It's hard to get down to the Macjack and there are just too many trees blocking the river to even consider heading down to its mouth." If some of these deadfalls were cleared, visitors would have the option of a river route to Raft Cove. The only other water access, known to ocean kayakers, is via the San Josef River and San Josef Bay.

The next time you visit the North Island, consider spending a day or so at Raft Cove Provincial Park. The hike in through the old-growth forest and along Raft Cove's beautiful sandy beach is worth the effort.

Contacts

Western Forest Products (Holberg) (604) 228-3362; B.C. Forest Service (Port McNeill) (604) 956-5000.

Maps/Guides

Western Forest Products Visitor's Guide to Northern Vancouver Island; B.C. Forest Service Port McNeill Forest District Recreation Map; Hiking Trails III (Outdoor Club of Victoria Trails Information Society); Canadian Tide and Current Tables: Vol. 6 (Canadian Hydrographic Service); National Topographical Series: 102I/9 San Josef (1:50,000); Provincial Map: 92L Alert Bay (1:125,000).

Nearest Services

Holberg.

Map Sources

CANADA MAP OFFICE
130 Bentley Avenue
Ottawa, ON
K1A 0E9
(613) 952-7000
FAX (613) 957-8861
(Federal maps/B.C. distributor list)

CANADIAN HYDROGRAPHIC SERVICE
Chart Sales & Distribution Office
Institute of Ocean Sciences
9860 West Saanich Road
P.O. Box 6000
Sidney, BC   V8L 4B2
(604) 363-6517
FAX (604) 363-6323
(tide books and marine charts)

GEOLOGICAL SURVEY OF CANADA
Sales Information Office
6th Floor, 100 West Pender St.
Vancouver, BC   V6B 1R0
(604) 666-0271
FAX (604) 666-1124
(Federal maps)

MAPS B.C.
Surveys and Mapping Branch
4th Floor, 1802 Douglas Street
Victoria, BC   V8V 1X4
(604) 387-1441
FAX (604) 387-3022
(Provincial maps and aerial photos)

WORLD WIDE BOOKS AND MAPS
949 Granville Street
Vancouver, BC
V6Z 1L3
(604) 687-3320
FAX (604) 687-5925

CANADIAN FOREST PRODUCTS LTD.
Englewood Division
Woss Camp, BC
V0N 3P0
(604) 281-2300
FAX (604) 281-2485

CROWN PUBLICATIONS
546 Yates Street
Victoria, BC
V8W 1K8
(604) 386-4636
FAX (604) 386-0221

EARTH QUEST BOOKS
1286 Broad Street
Victoria, BC
V8W 2A5
(604) 361-4533
(604) 386-4636
FAX (604) 386-0221

ISLAND BLUEPRINT
905 Fort Street
Victoria, BC
V8V 3K3
(604) 385-9786
FAX (604) 385-1377

ROBINSON'S SPORTING GOODS
1307 Broad Street
Victoria, BC
V8W 2A8
(604) 385-3429
FAX (604) 385-5835

B.C. FOREST SERVICE
Vancouver Forest Region
Regional Recreation Officer
4595 Canada Way
Burnaby, BC   V5G 4L9
(604) 660-7500
FAX (604) 660-7778

(B.C. Forest Service recreation maps
are available for the Duncan, Port
Alberni, Campbell River and Port
McNeill forest districts.)

CANADIAN PACIFIC FOREST PROD. LTD.
1000, 1040 West Georgia Street
Vancouver, BC
V6E 4K4
(604) 640-3400
FAX 684-1026

MACMILLAN BLOEDEL LTD.
925 West Georgia Street
Vancouver, BC
V6C 3L2
(604) 661-8000
(604) 661-8671 (Public Affairs)
FAX (604) 687-5345

FLETCHER CHALLENGE CANADA LTD.
P.O. Box 10058
Pacific Centre
Vancouver, BC V7L 1J7
(604) 654-4000
(604) 654-4050 (Public Affairs)
FAX (604) 654-4961

WESTERN FOREST PRODUCTS LTD.
Suite 1200
1140 West Pender Street
Vancouver, BC
V6E 4G6
(604) 665-6200
FAX (604) 665-6268

Other Useful Addresses

B.C. PARKS
2nd Floor
810 Johnson Street
Victoria, BC
V8V 1X4
(604) 387-5002
(604) 387-4609 (Public
Information Officer)
FAX (604) 387-5757

CAPITAL REGIONAL DISTRICT
Regional Parks Department
490 Atkins Avenue
Victoria, BC
V9B 2Z8
(604) 478-3344
FAX (604) 478-5416
(Many brochures on CRD
regional parks are available.)

REGIONAL DISTRICT OF MOUNT WADDINGTON
P.O. Box 729
Port McNeill, BC
V0N 2R0
(604) 956-3301
FAX (604) 956-3232

CAMPBELL RIVER SEARCH AND
    RESCUE SOCIETY
Box 705
Campbell River, BC
V9W 6J3
(Their logging and highway map
covers the Campbell River, Sayward,
Oyster River and Buttle Lake areas.)

OUTDOOR CLUB OF VICTORIA
TRAILS INFORMATION SOCIETY
c/o Sono Nis
1745 Blanshard Street
Victoria, BC   V8W 2J8
(Their Hiking Trails Vols. I, II & III
cover the Victoria area, southeastern
Vancouver Island and central and
northern Island trails, respectively.)

(A composite road map of the
North Island with detailed logging
roads is available for a total of $7.35,
including GST and postage.)

Seasonal forestry woods and mill tours are available in a number of regions on Vancouver Island. Information is available from:

NORTH ISLAND FORESTRY CENTRE (Beaver Cove) (604) 956-3844.
FORESTRY INFORMATION CENTRES: (Campbell River) (604) 286-3872;
  (Courtenay) (604) 334-1923; (Port Alberni) (604) 724-888; (Tofino)
  (604) 725-3295; (Lake Cowichan) (604) 749-3244.
WESTERN FOREST PRODUCTS (Jordan River) (604) 642-6351.

Anglers will be interested in the following publications, which give information on Island lakes, access roads and fishing opportunities:

Island Angler published monthly by Andrew Kolasinski.
Island Fish Finder Magazine published monthly by Rosebrugh Holdings Ltd.
Okay Anglers B.C. Fishing Directory & Atlas published annually by Art Belhumeur Ent. Ltd.
Steelhead & Freshwater Fishing Guide (Vancouver Island) published by Pacific Rim Publications.
The Lakes of Vancouver Island published by B.C. Environment (1988).

Suggested Reading

Akrigg, G.P.V. and Helen B., British Columbia Place Names, Victoria: Sono Nis, 1986.

Blier, Richard K., Island Adventures, An Outdoors Guide to Vancouver Island, Victoria: Orca Book Publishers, 1989.

Bruhn, Karl, Best of B.C. Lake Fishing, Vancouver/Toronto: Whitecap Books, 1992.

Bryson, Sandy, Vancouver Island Traveller, Juneau: Windham Bay Press, 1988.

Dowd, John. Sea Kayaking: A Manual for Long-Distance Touring, Vancouver: Douglas & McIntyre, 1986.

Guppy, Walter, Wet Coast Ventures, Mine-Finding on Vancouver Island, Victoria: Cappis Press, 1988.

Hall, Del, At The End of the Trail From Victoria, Victoria: Cougar Press Ltd., 1989.

Ince, John and Kottner, Hedi, Sea Kayaking Canada's West Coast, Vancouver: Raxas Books, 1982.

Merriman, Alec and Taffy, Logging Road Travel: Vols. I & II, Sidney: Saltaire Publ., 1977-79.

Meyer, Kathleen, How to Shit In The Woods, Berkeley: Ten Speed Press, 1989.

Obee, Bruce, The Pacific Rim Explorer, North Vancouver: Whitecap Books, 1986.

Nanton, Isabel and Simpson, Mary, Adventuring In British Columbia, Vancouver: Douglas & McIntyre, 1991.

Nicholson, George, Vancouver Island's West Coast 1762-1962, Vancouver: George Nicholson's Books, 1981.

Pacquet, Maggie, Parks of British Columbia and the Yukon, North Vancouver: Maia Publishing Ltd., 1990.

Pattison, Ken, *Milestones on Vancouver Island*, Victoria: Pattison Ventures Ltd., 1986.

Petersen, Lester R., *The Cape Scott Story*, Langley: Sunfire, 1985.

Pratt-Johnson, Betty, *Whitewater Trips for Kayakers, Canoeists and Rafters on Vancouver Island*, Vancouver: Soules Book Publishers, 1984.

Priest, Simon, *Bicycling Vancouver Island & The Gulf Islands*, Vancouver: Douglas & McIntyre, 1984.

Thomson, Richard E., *Oceanography of the British Columbia Coast*, Ottawa: Canadian Special Publication of Fisheries and Aquatic Sciences 56, 1984.

Sierra Club of B.C., *The West Coast Trail and Nitinat Lakes*, Vancouver: Douglas & McIntyre Ltd., 1985.

Sierra Club of B.C., *Victoria In a Knapsack*, Victoria: Sierra Club of B.C., 1985.

Snowden, Mary Ann, *Island Paddling*, Victoria: Orca Book Publishers, 1990.

Stoltmann, Randy, *Hiking Guide to the Big Trees of Southwestern British Columbia*, Vancouver: Western Canada Wilderness Committee, 1987.

Walbran, John T., *British Columbia Coast Names*, Vancouver: Douglas & McIntyre Ltd., 1977.

Watmough, Don, *Cruising Guide to British Columbia, Vol. IV: West Coast of Vancouver Island, Cape Scott to Sooke*, Vancouver: Maclean-Hunter Ltd., 1984.

Weston, Jim and Stirling, David, *The Naturalist's Guide to the Victoria Region*, Victoria: Victoria Natural History Society, 1986.

Note: Some of the above may be out-of-print.

Index

About the author

Richard K. Blier has travelled and photographed Vancouver Island backroads for over seventeen years. He is a feature writer for B.C. *Outdoors* magazine and has been a regular contributor to the Victoria *Times/Colonist* Sunday supplement, *The Islander*, since 1982. His first book, *Island Adventures*, was published in 1989.

Mr. Blier is an active member of the Outdoor Writers of Canada.

* author photo by Bill Hadden, courtesy of Studio '92 Photography